D0533859

driving
goods vehicles
he official DSA syllabus

Approved by
Plain
English
Campaign

SANDWELL LIBRARIES

I 1831461

London: TSO

Published with the permission of the Driving Standards Agency on behalf of the Controller of Her Majesty's Stationery Office.

© Crown Copyright 2003

All right reserved. Applications for reproduction should be made in writing to Commercial Department, Driving Standards Agency, Stanley House, 56 Talbot Street, Nottingham NG1 5GU

First edition Crown copyright 1994
Seventh edition Crown copyright 2005
ISBN 0 11 552656 0

A CIP catalogue record for this book is available from the British Library

Other titles in the official Driving Series

The Official Theory Test for Drivers of Larg[

The Official Theory Test (CD-Rom) for Driv[

Driving Buses and Coaches – the Official [

The Official Guide to Tractor and Specialis[

The Official Theory Test for Car Drivers

The Official Theory Test (CD-Rom) for Car [

The Official Theory Test for Motorcyclists

The Official Theory Test (CD-Rom) for Moto[

The Official Guide to Learning to Drive (for[

Driving - the essential skills

Official Motorcycling – CBT, Theory and Practical Test

Motorcycle Riding – the essential skills

The Official Guide to Helping Learners to Practise

Learning to Drive (DVD)

The Official Guide to Hazard Perception (DVD)

Roadsense - Hazard Perception (VHS)

SANDWELL LIBRARY & INFORMATION	
I 1831461	
CO	26/08/2005
629.2844	14.99

Every effort has been made to ensure that the information in this publication is accurate at the time of going to press. The Stationery Office cannot be held responsible for any inaccuracies. Please check that you have the most up-to-date version available. All metric and imperial conversions in this book are approximate.

Information and advice contained within this publication is for guidance only. Vehicle maintenance or other tasks must be carried out only with careful reference to an individual vehicle's handbook and any safety information relating to the vehicle. Close regard must also be had to the health and safety of those undertaking such tasks and any others who might be affected by this.

Please note that individual commercial organisations may prohibit their employees from carrying out some or all of the maintenance or other tasks described in this publication and users are advised to check with their employers before attempting such tasks.

The Driving Standards Agency (DSA) is an executive agency of the Department for Transport (DfT).   You'll see its logo at test centres.

DSA aims to promote road safety through the advancement of driving standards, by

- establishing and developing high standards and best practice in driving and riding on the road; before people start to drive, as they learn, and after they pass their test
- ensuring high standards of instruction for different types of driver and rider
- conducting the statutory theory and practical tests efficiently, fairly and consistently across the country
- providing a centre of excellence for driver training and driving standards
- developing a range of publications and other publicity material designed to promote safe driving for life.

Driving Standards Agency recognises and values its customers. We will treat all our customers with respect, and deliver our services in an objective, polite and fair manner.

As a Trading Fund, we are required to cover our costs from the driving test fee. We do not have a quota for test passes or fails and if you demonstrate the standard required, you will pass your test.

DSA website

www.driving-tests.co.uk

DfT website

www.dft.gov.uk

Green Issues Website

www.defra.gov.uk/environment/index.htm

Acknowledgements

The Driving Standards Agency (DSA) would like to thank the following organisations for their contribution to the production of this publication

Association of Police Officers in Scotland

Buckinghamshire Fire and Rescue Service

The Confederation of Passenger Transport UK

County Durham and Darlington Fire and Rescue Brigade

Department for Transport

Driver and Vehicle Licensing Agency

Driver and Vehicle Testing Agency Northern Ireland

ETA Services Ltd

London Borough Cycle Officers

Road Haulage and Distribution Training Council

Road Haulage Association

The Traffic Director for London

Transport Licensing and Enforcement Branch, Department of Environment Northern Ireland

As the driver of a large goods vehicle (LGV) you have a special responsibility – not just to yourself, but to all other road users. A professional driver should set an example to other drivers by ensuring that the vehicle is driven, at all times, with the utmost safety and with courtesy and consideration for everyone else on today's busy roads.

To become an LGV driver you must possess a high degree of skill in the handling of your vehicle and also be prepared to make allowances for the behaviour of others. The right attitude and approach to your driving, together with a sound knowledge of professional driving techniques and the ability to apply those techniques, are essential.

By successfully passing your car driving test you've already shown that you've reached the standard set for driving a motor vehicle unsupervised on today's roads. This book sets out the skills that you must now show in order to pass the vocational driving test. Put the information it contains into practice and you should be able to reach the higher standards demanded. From there you could earn the privilege of driving large goods vehicles and, above all, go on to a career of 'Safe driving for life'.

Robin Cummins

Robin Cummins

Chief Driving Examiner

Driving Standards Agency

This book will help you to

- understand what a large goods vehicle (LGV) driver needs to know to be thoroughly professional
- prepare for the range of skills you'll need to show to pass your practical LGV driving test.

Part One tells you how to get started. Here you'll also learn about the difference between driving lorries and cars. The importance of driver attitudes and different vehicle characteristics are also covered.

Part Two will help you understand LGVs, how different forces affect your handling of the vehicle, also how different types of LGVs need to be handled in order to drive them safely. Details on vehicle limits, braking systems and load restraints are all explained.

Part Three explains how the environment is affected by LGVs and what you as a professional driver can do to help reduce the detrimental impact. Legal requirements and other regulations are also covered within this section.

Part Four tells the potential professional driver about driving in different weather conditions, at night and on motorways. Information on dealing with congestion is also included, along with more advice on green issues. It also gives helpful advice about dealing with accidents and emergencies. The first aid section explains how you can give assistance whilst waiting for the emergency services. It also looks at the essential skills you'll need to drive professionally.

Part Five contains the official syllabus for learning to drive an LGV and shows the skills you need to learn before taking your test.

Part Six explains the test requirements fully and provides clear advice. Refer to it regularly and use it to check your progress.

Part Seven gives additional useful information and addresses.

The important factors

This book is only **one** of the important factors in your training. Other factors are

- a good instructor
- plenty of practice
- your attitude.

If you're driving an LGV you must ensure that your goods arrive at their destination safely. This process will not only involve the safety of your load, but also your attitude to others on the road. From the start, you must be aware of the differences between driving small and large vehicles.

To become a professional driver you must have a thorough knowledge of the regulations that apply to your work.

It's also vitally important that you have the correct training and instruction from the start.

Large Goods Vehicle Voluntary Register

DSA launched the voluntary register of LGV instructors in April 1997.

The register was developed by DSA working in close conjuction with freight and haulage associations and those in the training organisations.

The aim of the scheme is to raise the standard of training for lorry drivers and so help to reduce accidents.

Ministers have announced that shortly the scheme will become compulsory.

For further information about the voluntary register or, if you would like to take instruction with a DSA registered LGV instructor, please contact the:

LGV Register Section
Driving Standards Agency
Stanley House
56 Talbot Street
Nottingham
NG5 1GU
Tel: 0115 901 2625/2626.

If you are already the holder of a full LGV licence and have held it for the appropriate length of time to accompany a provisional LGV driver, you may be interested in joining the Register yourself. For more information contact the LGV Register section.

Study materials

You should already have a good, sound knowledge of driving skills. It's strongly recommended that you study a copy of *The Highway Code*. You can buy one from any good bookshop or newsagent. It can also be found on a dedicated website, www.highwaycode.gov.uk.

The Highway Code is also available together with the *Theory Test Companion*, which summarises the contents of the theory test for car drivers.

The DSA series of books (see page ii) will provide you with the information you need to further your skills and knowledge. *Driving - the Essential Skills* and *The Official Theory Test for Drivers of Large Vehicles* are particularly recommended.

A DVD entitled *The official guide to hazard perception* for all drivers and riders will help candidates prepare for the hazard perception part of the theory test. A video and workbook-based training pack entitled *Roadsense* is also available. These are also very useful tools for existing drivers wanting to brush up on their hazard awareness skills.

All the above publications can be bought from some retail outlets and from DSA Merchandising, tel. 0870 241 4523.

3

Part One

Getting Started

The topics covered

- Selecting an instructor
- Applying for your licence
- The theory test
- Medical requirements
- Professional standards
- Responsibility and attitude

Selecting an instructor

It is important that you have the correct training and instruction before taking your LGV test.

DSA has developed a voluntary register of instructors (more details on page 2). If you would like to take instruction from a registered instructor, contact

The LGV Register Section
Driving Standards Agency
Stanley House
56 Talbot Street
Nottingham
NG5 1GU
Tel: 0115 901 2625/2626

Applying for your licence

You should apply to the Driver and Vehicle Licensing Agency (DVLA) in Swansea for the provisional entitlement to drive large goods vehicles (LGVs). An application form D1 is available from post offices.

In order to drive an LGV you must

- have a full driving licence for a category B vehicle
- hold a provisional LGV driving licence in the category that you wish to drive
- meet the eyesight and medical requirements
- normally be over 21 years old, unless you're a member of the armed forces authorised by the Ministry of Defence or a registered trainee within the Young Large Goods Vehicle (LGV) Driver Training Scheme.

Full details can be obtained from the DVLA enquiry line, 0870 240 0009, or from The Road Haulage and Distribution Training Council on 01908 313360 (www.rhdtc.co.uk).

If you passed your car driving test after 1 January 1997 and want to drive a vehicle between 3.5 and 7.5 tonnes you'll have to take a medium-sized lorry test (category C1) and meet the higher medical standards.

Automatic transmission

If your vehicle doesn't have a clutch pedal, it's classed as an 'automatic'. If you take the LGV driving test in an automatic vehicle, your full LGV licence will restrict you to driving only LGVs fitted with automatic transmission.

Some modern vehicles have transmission systems where sensors select the next gear without the driver using the clutch pedal. These are also classed as 'automatic'.

Articulated vehicles

You must already hold a full licence to drive a rigid large goods vehicle (C1 or C) before you can apply for a provisional licence to drive an articulated vehicle (C1 + E or C + E). You don't have to pass a test in category C1 before taking a test in category C.

By then you'll already have experience of driving large vehicles. The information in this book about driving articulated vehicles will help you to prepare for your test and learn how to deal with the various characteristics of this type of vehicle.

If you're taking your test with a trailer you'll be expected to demonstrate uncoupling and recoupling during your test.

The theory test

All new drivers wishing to drive large goods vehicles (LGVs) will have to pass a theory test before taking a practical driving test. You can start your lessons before passing the theory test but you must pass before a booking for a practical test can be accepted. The theory test pass certificate has a 2-year life. If the practical test isn't passed within that time, the theory test will have to be re-taken. When you receive your provisional licence you must

• sign it.

When driving as a learner you must

• be accompanied by a qualified driver who has held a full licence for the category of vehicle being driven for at least 3 years

• display L plates (or D plates, if you wish, when driving in Wales) to the front and rear of the vehicle.

You'll have to be fully qualified in a lower category of entitlement before seeking to gain entitlement in a higher category or sub-category. You'll have to

• pass a category C test before taking a category C + E test

• pass a category C or C1 test before taking a category C1 + E test.

You won't have to gain a C1 before taking a test in category C.

Medical requirements

Eyesight

All drivers must be able to read, in good daylight, a number plate at 20.5 metres (about 67 feet), or 20 metres (about 66 feet) if the new narrow font letters have been used on the number plate. If you need to wear glasses or contact lenses to perform this test, these must be worn while driving.

If you are applying for an LGV or PCV licence for the first time you must by law have a visual acuity of at least

- 6/9 in the better eye
- 6/12 in the other eye

wearing glasses or contact lenses, if needed. You must also have an uncorrected visual acuity of at least 3/60 in each eye.

The visual field requirement is the normal binocular field of vision.

Drivers who held an LGV/PCV licence before 1 January 1997 but who don't meet the new standard may still qualify for a licence.

If you require any further general information you should contact DVLA on 0870 240 0009.

For enquiries about medical standards you should contact the

Drivers Medical Group
DVLA
Swansea
SA99 1TU

Tel: 0870 600 0301.

If you normally wear glasses or contact lenses, always wear them whenever you drive.

Medical examination and form D4

Driving an LGV carries a heavy responsibility towards all other road users so it's vital that you meet exacting medical standards.

Consult your doctor first if you have any doubts about your fitness. In any case, if this is your first application for LGV entitlement, a medical report must be completed by a doctor. You'll also need to send in a medical report with your application if you're renewing your LGV licence and you're aged 45 or over, unless you've already sent one during the last 12 months.

You'll need to have a medical examination in order to complete form D4.

Only complete the applicant details and declaration (Section 8 on the form) when you're with your doctor at the time of the examination. Your doctor will complete the other sections. The medical report will cover

- vision
- nervous system
- diabetes mellitus
- psychiatric illness
- general health
- cardiac health
- medical practitioner details.

Study the notes on pages 1 and 2 of form D4 then remove these two pages before sending in your application and keep them for future reference.

This medical report isn't available free under National Health rules. Your doctor is entitled to charge the current fee for this report. You're responsible for paying this fee: it can't be recovered from DVLA. In addition, the fee isn't refundable if your application is refused.

The completed form must be received by DVLA within four months of the date of your doctor's signature.

Change in health

It's your responsibility to notify immediately the Drivers Medical Unit at DVLA, Swansea, if you have or develop any serious illness or disability that's likely to last more than three months and which could affect your driving.

Medical standards

You may be refused an LGV driving licence if you suffer from any of the following

- liability to epilepsy*/seizure
- diabetes requiring insulin (unless you held a licence on 1 April 1991 and the Traffic Commissioner who issued that licence had knowledge of your condition)
- eyesight defects (see the eyesight requirements on page 7)
- heart disorders
- persistent high blood pressure (see the notes on form D4 for details)
- a stroke within the past year
- unconscious lapses within the last five years
- any disorder causing vertigo within the last year
- severe head injury, with serious continuing after-effects, or major brain surgery
- Parkinson's disease, multiple sclerosis or other chronic nervous disorders likely to affect the use of the limbs
- mental disorders
- alcohol/drug problems
- serious difficulty in communicating by telephone in an emergency.

*Note
A driver who remains seizure free for at least 10 years (without anticonvulsant treatment within that time) may be eligible for a licence but with restricted entitlement. Contact DVLA for further information.

Professional standards

Driving an LGV requires skill combined with knowledge and the right attitude and driving techniques.

To become a professional driver you'll need

- the demanding driving skills required
- the knowledge to deal with all the regulations that apply to your work
- a comprehensive knowledge of *The Highway Code* including the meaning of traffic signs and road markings, especially those which indicate a restriction for LGVs.

From the start, you'll need to appreciate the differences between driving small and large goods vehicles. It's also essential to understand the forces at work on your vehicle and its load.

Initially, the most important thing to learn is that the way you drive is vital.

- Drive properly and safely and the goods entrusted into your care will arrive safely at their destination.
- Drive dangerously or even carelessly, and the potential for disaster is enormous.

Whether you're driving an unladen lorry of 7.5 tonnes or a fully laden articulated vehicle of 38 tonnes or more, you can never act hastily without serious consequences resulting.

No risk is ever justified

Responsibility and attitude

A loaded LGV travelling at speed and colliding with another vehicle will cause serious damage. You're the one with the responsibility of driving your vehicle safely at all times.

Your vehicle will probably have the owner's name on display, and so your driving will be similarly on display. Make sure that your vehicle is clean and well maintained, and that your driving reaches the same high standards. Show a good example of skill, courtesy and tolerance to other road users. Be a credit to yourself, your company and your profession.

Your LGV licence is a privilege which requires effort to gain and even more effort to keep.

Appropriate behaviour

As a professional driver you should set a good example of driving to others. You should always have an idea of how other road users see you. Be aware that they might not understand why you take up certain positions to make turns or take longer to manoeuvre.

You'll spend a great deal of time at the wheel of your vehicle. Losing your temper or having a bad attitude towards other road users won't make your working life pleasant. A good attitude will help you to enjoy your work and is safer for others around you.

Tailgating

The sheer size, noise and appearance of a typical LGV often appears somewhat intimidating to a cyclist, motorcyclist or even the average car driver. Travelling dangerously close behind a smaller vehicle at speed can be very intimidating for the vehicle in front. When an LGV appears to be being driven in an aggressive way other road users often feel really threatened.

If you drive too close to the vehicle in front, your view of the road ahead may be severely restricted. You may not be able to see or plan for any hazards that might occur. The room in which you have to stop is also reduced, probably to less than the stopping distance for the speed at which you're travelling. This is a dangerous practice.

Police forces are concerned at the number of accidents that are caused as a direct result of vehicles driving much too close to each other. A number have mounted campaigns to video and prosecute offenders.

In an effort to improve the image of the transport industry some large retail organisations are reviewing the placing of contracts with any distributor whose vehicles have been seen repeatedly tailgating on motorways.

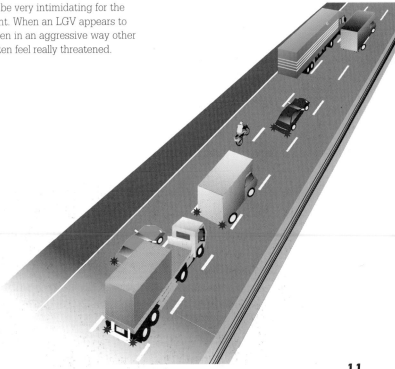

Intimidation

Don't use the size, weight and power of your vehicle to intimidate other road users. Even the repeated 'hiss' from air brakes being applied while stationary gives the impression of 'breathing down the neck' of the driver in front.

Speed

The introduction of 'just in time' flow-line policies reduces the need for manufacturers to hold large stocks of materials. These policies are also intended to ensure the delivery of fresh foods at the supermarket, for example.

Don't allow your employer to set delivery targets which are unrealistic. You should never be under extreme pressure to meet deadlines.

You can never justify driving too fast simply because you need to reach a given location by a specific time, whether it be a ferry, loading bay or depot.

If an accident results and you injure someone, there's no possible defence for your actions.

Retaliation

You should resist, at all times, impatience or the temptation to retaliate. Always drive

- courteously
- with anticipation
- calmly, allowing for other road users' mistakes
- with full control of your vehicle.

You can't act hastily without the possibility of serious loss of control when driving an LGV.

An LGV 'towering' over a car

The horn

Because LGVs are often equipped with powerful multi-tone air horns, their use should be strictly confined to the guidance set out in *The Highway Code* – to warn other road users of your presence.

See page 97 for more information about using the horn.

The headlights

To avoid dazzle don't switch the headlights on to full beam when following another vehicle.

Don't

- switch on additional auxiliary lights that may be fitted to your vehicle unless the weather conditions require their use (they must be switched off when the weather improves)
- repeatedly flash the headlights while driving directly behind another vehicle.

Flashing the headlights lets other road users know that you're there.

It doesn't mean that you wish to give or take priority. You may be misunderstood by others when using an unauthorised code of headlight flashing, which could lead to accidents.

Neither the headlights nor the horn(s) must be used to rebuke or to intimidate another road user. Courtesy and consideration are the hallmarks of a professional driver.

Mobile phones

It is illegal to use a hand-held mobile phone whilst driving. Using hands-free equipment can also distract your attention from the road. Do not accept calls whilst driving, wait until you are able to find a safe place to stop before answering.

Driving a large goods vehicle requires all of your attention, all of the time.

You're four times
It's hard to
more likely to have
concentrate on
a road accident
two things
when you're on
at the same time.
a mobile phone.

THINK!
Switch it off when you drive.

Effects of your vehicle

As a competent LGV driver you must always be aware of the effect your vehicle and your driving has on other road users.

You need to recognise the effects of turbulence or buffeting caused by your vehicle, especially when passing

- pedestrians
- horse riders (on the road or grass verge)
- cyclists
- motorcyclists
- cars
- cars towing caravans
- other lorries and buses.

On congested built-up roads, particularly in shopping areas, take extra care when you need to drive closer to the kerb. Be aware of

- the possibility of a pedestrian stepping off the kerb (and under the wheels)
- the nearside mirror striking the head of a pedestrian standing at the edge of the kerb
- cyclists moving up the nearside of your vehicle in slow-moving traffic.

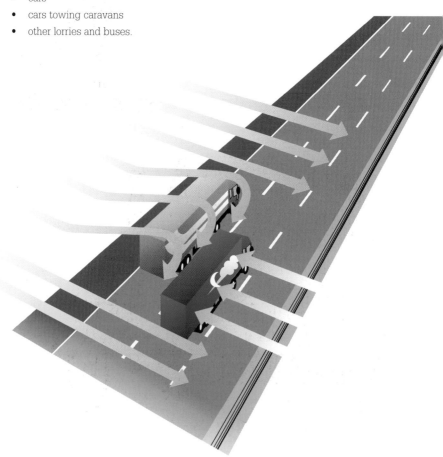

Cyclists

Over a quarter of cyclist deaths are as a result of collisions with LGVs. You need to be aware of the limited vision you have around your vehicle due to its size and shape. Use your mirrors so that you have a constant picture of what's happening all around. Always check any blind spots before you move away.

Also remember that cyclists could become unbalanced by the buffeting effect of a large vehicle passing closely.

Part Two

Understanding large goods vehicles

The topics covered

- Understanding LGVs
- Forces affecting your vehicle
- Vehicle characteristics
- Vehicle limits
- Vehicle maintenance
- Load restraint

Understanding LGVs

You'll need to study and understand the information given in this book before you can consider taking an LGV driving test. You also need to understand how various kinds of LGVs handle in order to drive them safely.

To drive a lorry safely you must first appreciate the main differences between driving small and large goods vehicles.

These are

- weight
- width
- length
- height
- distance needed to pull up
- distance needed to overtake
- control needed when going downhill
- power needed to climb uphill
- the need to avoid any sudden changes of speed or direction.

Some of these aspects will be obvious from the moment you first start to drive an LGV. Other features will only become apparent after you've gained experience. The essential factor is to recognise that much more forward planning and anticipation is needed to drive an LGV safely.

Whether an LGV is

- laden or unladen
- rigid
- towing a drawbar trailer
- articulated

it's most stable when travelling in a straight line under gentle acceleration. Sudden or violent

- steering
- acceleration
- braking

can cause severe loss of control. All braking should be carried out smoothly and in good time.

Most modern large vehicles are fitted with an air braking system. Older vehicles might have a hydraulic braking system. In **this** case, if you find you need to 'pump' the brakes, **stop** as safely as you can in a convenient place and check the hydraulic system. Don't drive on unless you're sure that you can stop safely.

Erratic handling

Sudden acceleration forward might cause an insecure load to fall off the back of a vehicle. Similarly, if harsh braking is applied

- the load may attempt to continue moving forward
- the tyres may lose their grip on the road surface causing the vehicle to skid
- the weight of the vehicle is transferred forward causing the front of the vehicle to 'dip' downward.

Any sudden steering movement may also unsettle the load and cause it to move. Any movement of the load is likely to make the vehicle unstable.

All acceleration and braking should be controlled and as smooth and progressive as possible.

Friction

The grip between two surfaces is due to friction. The grip that rubber tyres have on a road surface produces traction (force), which enables a vehicle to

- move away or accelerate
- turn/change direction
- brake/slow down.

The amount of friction, and hence traction, will depend on

- the weight of the vehicle
- the vehicle's speed
- the condition of the tyre tread
- the tyre pressure

- the type and condition of the road surface
  - anti-skid
  - loose
  - smooth
- weather conditions
- any other material present on the road
  - mud
  - wet leaves
  - diesel spillage
  - other slippery spillages
  - inset metal rail lines
- the rate of change of speed or direction (sudden steering/ braking)
- the condition of mechanical components
  - steering alignment
  - suspension.

Sudden acceleration or deceleration can reduce the grip your vehicle has on the road. Under these conditions the vehicle may

- lose traction (wheelspin)
- break away on a turn (skid)
- not stop safely (skid)
- overturn.

Jack-knifing

This is usually more likely to occur with an unladen vehicle.

In the case of an articulated vehicle, severe braking can result in jack-knifing as the tractive unit is pushed by the semi-trailer pivoting around the coupling (fifth wheel). This is even more likely if the vehicle isn't travelling in a straight line when the brakes are applied.

Similar results will occur with a drawbar trailer, where there may be **two** pivoting points: at the coupling pin and at the turntable of the front wheels of a two- or more axle trailer.

Changing into a lower gear when travelling at too high a speed or releasing the clutch suddenly can produce much the same effect, as the braking effect is only applied to the driven wheels.

For some years now, well-proven systems have been available that reduce the risk of jack-knifing on articulated vehicles.

Some vehicles are equipped with retarders, a sophisticated electronic system, that ensures appropriate braking effort is applied to the trailer wheels.

Trailer swing

This can occur on a drawbar combination (or occasionally on an articulated unit) when

- sharp braking is applied on a bend
- excessive steering takes place at speed
- the brakes on either the tractive unit or trailer aren't properly adjusted.

It follows that all braking, gear changes, steering and acceleration should be smooth and under full control.

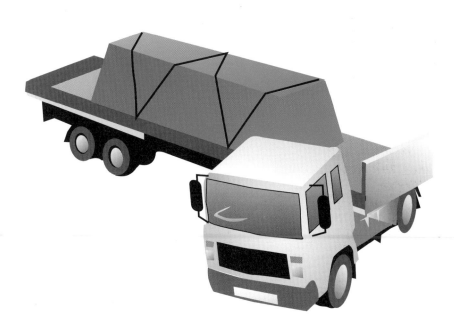

Forces affecting your vehicle

Gravity

When a vehicle is stationary on level ground the only force generally acting upon it (ignoring wind forces, etc.) is the downward pull of gravity.

On an uphill gradient gravity will have a greater effect on a moving vehicle and its load so that

- more power is needed from the engine to move the vehicle and its load forward and upward

- less braking effort is needed and the vehicle will pull up in a shorter distance.

On a downhill gradient the effect of gravity will tend to

- make the vehicle's speed increase
- require more braking effort
- increase stopping distances.

A vehicle's centre of gravity is the point around which all of its weight is balanced. To keep the vehicle and its load stable this should be arranged to be

- as low as possible
- along a line running centrally down the length of the LGV.

The higher this centre of gravity occurs, the less stable a vehicle and/or its load will be. As a result the vehicle will become more easily affected by

- braking
- steering
- the slope (camber) of a road
- the wheels running over a kerb and resulting in either the load tilting or falling, or the vehicle overturning.

End-tipper vehicles

When a loaded tipper vehicle body (whether tanker, bulk carrier or high-sided open body) is raised to discharge a load, the centre of gravity is raised to a critical position. It's vitally important to ensure that the vehicle is on a level, solid surface before engaging the hoist mechanism.

Ensure that there are no overhead power lines in the vicinity. Keep clear of scaffolding or any other obstructions.

Side-tipper vehicles

Always select the firmest level site available before tilting the vehicle body. Until the load is discharged, all the weight will be transferred to one side. Unless the vehicle is on firm level ground there is a risk of it overturning.

Always take the time to check the ground before tipping. Get out and check all around the vehicle. Make sure that it's safe before you tip.

Kinetic energy

This is the energy held by a moving vehicle. The amount depends on the

- mass (weight) of the vehicle plus its load
- speed.

Kinetic energy must be reduced by the brakes in order to stop a vehicle. The kinetic energy of a stationary vehicle is zero.

An increase in speed from 15 mph to 45 mph (× 3) increases the kinetic energy **ninefold** (3 × 3). If you reduce the speed by half, say from 50 mph to 25 mph, the kinetic energy acting on your vehicle is **one-quarter** of what it was before braking.

As the brakes reduce the speed of a vehicle, kinetic energy is converted into heat. Continuous use of the brakes can result in them becoming overheated and losing their effectiveness, especially on long downhill gradients. This is known as 'brake fade'.

The effort required to stop a fully laden LGV travelling at 56 mph (90 km/h) is so much greater than that needed to stop an ordinary motor car travelling at similar speed. You'll need to allow extra time and space to stop an LGV safely. Don't follow other vehicles too closely – always leave a safe separation distance. In addition, harsh braking should be avoided at all times when driving an LGV.

Momentum

This is the tendency for a vehicle and/or its load to continue in a straight line. It depends on

- mass (weight)
- speed.

The higher the speed, the greater the momentum and the greater the effort required to

- stop
- change direction.

Centrifugal force

When a vehicle takes a curved path at a bend the force acting upon it will tend to cause the vehicle to leave the road at a tangent to the bend. At low speeds this force will be overcome by the traction of the tyres on the road surface.

If a loaded vehicle takes a bend at too high a speed the centrifugal force acting on it may cause it to become unstable and may also cause the load to become detached and fall off the side.

Forces on the load

If the forces acting on a load cause it to become detached from the vehicle, the load will move in the direction of the force. While

- accelerating, it will fall off the back
- braking, it will continue moving forward
- tilting, it will topple over
- turning, it will continue on the original path and fall off the side.

Loss of control

You can ask too much of your tyres if you turn and brake at the same time at too high a speed. Once any or all the tyres lift or slide (that is, they lose traction) you're no longer in control of the vehicle. What happens next will depend on the particular forces that are acting on the vehicle.

When any change is made to a vehicle's motion or direction the same forces will act on any load being carried, therefore that load needs to be secured to the vehicle so that it can't move.

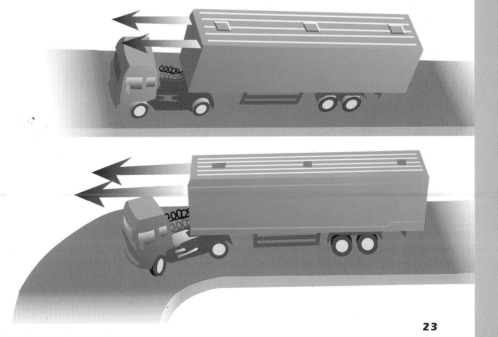

Shedding loads

There are several differences between driving a large vehicle and driving a smaller vehicle or a car. An unladen vehicle will handle differently from a laden one. Handling will also change depending on the size or type of load carried.

The following can lead to the shedding of a load.

- Driving error
  - sudden change of speed or direction
  - too high a speed
  - skidding.

- Instability of load
  - unsuitable vehicle
  - badly stowed
  - movement in load
  - restraints failed
  - unsuitable type of restraint.

- Mechanical failure
  - suspension failure
  - tyre failure
  - trailer disengaged
  - wheel loss.

- Collision
  - another vehicle
  - a bridge, etc.
  - lamp-posts
  - signs
  - signals
  - bollards.

Most of these situations are preventable.

You should know the handling characteristics of the vehicle that you're driving and drive in a safe and sensible manner.

Maintaining control

You can't alter the severity of a bend or change the weight of a load. However, you do have control over the **speed** and **braking** of your vehicle.

Reduce speed in good time, by braking if necessary, before negotiating

- bends
- roundabouts
- corners.

To keep control you should ensure that all braking is

- controlled
- in good time
- made when travelling in a straight line, wherever possible.

Avoid braking and turning at the same time (unless manoeuvring at low speed). Look **well** ahead to assess and plan.

Vehicle characteristics

The different types of large goods vehicles will each require specific handling. You'll need to bear this in mind if you want to become a professional LGV driver.

Short-wheelbase vehicles

These

- will bounce more noticeably than some long-wheelbase vehicles when empty (This can affect braking efficiency and all-round control)
- shouldn't be pushed into bends or corners at higher speeds simply because the vehicle appears to be easier to drive.

Long-wheelbase rigid vehicles

These require additional room to manoeuvre, especially

- when turning left or right
- negotiating roundabouts
- entering or leaving premises.

Typical examples of this type of vehicle are

- removal vans
- box vans
- brick carriers
- bulk carriers (for aggregates, etc.)
- 'eight-wheeler' tankers.

Box vans

In addition to the extra space needed when turning, the box type of body, when lightly loaded or empty, is very susceptible to crosswinds on exposed stretches of road. Failure to heed adverse weather warnings may well result in the vehicle being blown over. For this reason, high-sided vehicles are often banned from using certain roads and bridges where these problems are known to occur.

It's essential to observe any temporary speed limits imposed during these conditions.

Articulated vehicles

Drivers of these vehicles should be especially vigilant before turning corners or negotiating roundabouts.

Failure to plan ahead and select the correct course might result in the rear wheels 'cutting in'. This could cause your vehicle to

- clip the kerb
- collide with street furniture.

It could also endanger

- pedestrians
- cyclists
- other vehicles.

You should avoid overshooting left or right turns.

The stability of the vehicle is at risk if an excessive steering lock is applied in order to make a 'swan-neck' turn.

Articulated tankers

The vehicle wheels on the inside of a curve may start to lift if the

- centre of gravity is high enough
- speed is high enough
- vehicle is travelling sufficiently fast
- vehicle is driven on a curved path.

In many cases this is followed seconds later by 'roll-over'.

The problem frequently involves tanker vehicles carrying fluids in bulk. The reasons for this problem have been attributed to a number of possible causes.

It appears most likely to occur when modern, heavier and more powerful vehicles (and, in the majority of cases, those equipped with power steering) reach a critical situation. As an example, the forces acting on a typical loaded articulated tanker vehicle negotiating a roundabout at a speed of about 25 mph will cause it to overturn if only a further quarter turn is applied to the steering wheel.

You must be fully alert to the possibility of this happening. Adjust the speed of your vehicle to avoid wheel-lift and roll-over.

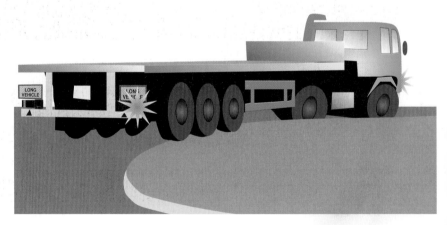

Roll-over

The type of suspension fitted to a vehicle will influence its resistance to roll-over.

Modern tri-axle semi-trailers fitted with single wheels on each side have extended the tracking width available, compared to twin-wheeled units, and hence have improved resistance to roll-over.

Although vehicles equipped with air suspension systems are often considered to possess improved anti-roll stability compared to traditional steel-leaf spring suspension, test results have shown that there are similarities in their level of stability.

Large petrochemical companies include specialised driver training within their training schemes to avoid such incidents happening.

The wave effect

If the drivers of certain tanker vehicles relax the footbrake when braking to a stop there's a danger that the motion in the fluid load could force their vehicles forward. This is due to the wave effect created in the tank contents, especially where baffle plates are omitted from the tank design. (Such tanks are sometimes found on vehicles carrying foodstuffs or where cleaning out the tanks presents difficulties).

Using walkways

Drivers of tanker vehicles must exercise special care when climbing onto walkways to gain access to tank hatches. Not only is this to avoid injury as a result of slipping off, but also to avoid the danger of overhead cables, pipeways, etc.

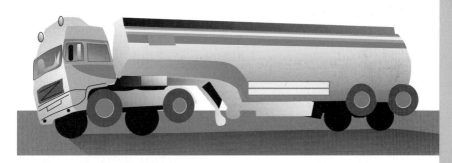

Venting

All tanks must be vented according to instructions. This will avoid serious damage to the tanker body as the external air pressure becomes greater than the pressure within the tank.

Compressed gases

Drivers of vehicles carrying compressed gases, especially at low temperatures (e.g., liquid nitrogen, oxygen, etc.), must comply with regulations relating to the transport of such materials.

Dangerous Goods

Drivers of vehicles carrying dangerous goods may need to hold a vocational training certificate.

Fire or explosion

In the case of vehicles carrying dangerous goods, all safety precautions must be strictly followed, especially where there's a risk of fire or explosion.

The electrical systems of vehicles carrying petrochemicals and other highly inflammable materials are modified to meet stringent safety requirements. No unauthorised additions or alterations must be made to such vehicles. Any defects must be reported immediately.

The appropriate fire-fighting equipment must be available and drivers trained in its use.

Articulated car transporters

These vehicles require even higher standards of driving and anticipation by the driver.

The overhang created by the top deck swings through a greater arc than the cab of the tractor unit, particularly when negotiating turns. This means that there's a risk of collision with

- traffic signals
- lamp-posts on central refuges
- traffic signs
- walls and buildings.

You should plan ahead and take an appropriate avoiding line on approach to turns when driving these vehicles.

The stability of these vehicles also needs to be considered. It's a case of last on, first off, so the lower deck may be clear of vehicles while there may be several still on top. The centre of gravity is substantially shifted in such cases.

You should be aware of the height of your vehicle at all times, especially if you're carrying vans.

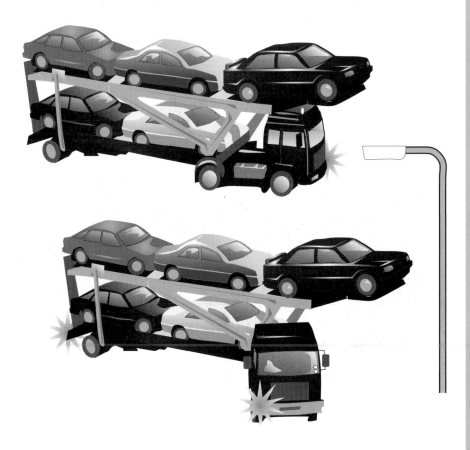

Demountable bodies

This type of vehicle is similar to a container, except that the body is fitted with 'legs', which can be lowered to enable the carrier vehicle to drive under or out.

Care needs to be taken to ensure that the

- legs are secured in the down position before the vehicle is driven out
- legs are secured in the up position before the vehicle moves off
- height is correct and the body is stable before driving the carrier vehicle underneath
- surface is firm and level before 'demounting' the body.

Another type (often an open, bulk high-sided body) is fitted with skids and is winched up onto the carrying vehicle. Apart from the dangers of overloading, care must be taken when operating such winches.

The construction of these vehicles often means that the centre of gravity can be higher than normal when conveying a loaded skip. Take this into account, especially when cornering.

Double-decked bodies

These vehicles are constructed to give increased carrying capacity to box van or curtain-side bodies. They're frequently used in the garment distribution sector.

Care must be taken to ensure that when the vehicle is in transit the lower deck isn't left empty while a load remains on the top tier. Such a shift in the centre of gravity will result in the high-sided vehicle being even more vulnerable in high winds and therefore, more likely to overturn.

Refrigerated vehicles

When driving refrigerated or 'reefer' vehicles carrying suspended meat carcasses, care must be taken to avoid the 'pendulum' effect when cornering. Always reduce speed in good time.

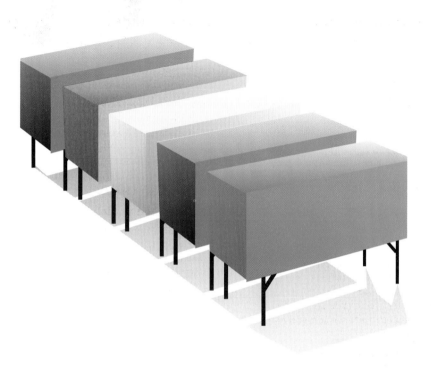

Vehicle limits

The transport industry is subject to an extremely large number of regulations and requirements relating to

- drivers
- operators
- companies
- vehicles
- goods.

It's essential that you keep up to date with all the changes in road transport legislation that affect you.

The first thing you'll need to know about is your vehicle. The various aspects to consider are its

- weight (restrictions)
- height (clearances, etc.)
- width (restrictions)
- length (clearances)
- ground clearance (low-loader or dual-purpose trailers only).

You'll also need to know the speed limits that apply to your vehicle and the speed at which it will normally travel.

Weight

It's essential that you're aware of, and understand, the limits relating to any vehicle that you drive. (Definitions of terms relating to weight limits can be found in the glossary of terms in Part Seven.)

Weight limits in many cases refer to the maximum gross weight (MGW) or the maximum authorised mass (MAM). You can drive heavier vehicles if engaged in inter-modal operations between road and rail terminals. These are subject to a number of conditions

- the number of axles
- tyre specifications
- axle spacings
- road-friendly suspension.

Also, special documentation is required to cover such movements between rail-head and road depot.

Road-friendly suspension generally means that an axle is fitted with air suspension, or a suspension regarded as being equivalent to air suspension (EC directive 92/7/EEC). At least 75 per cent of the spring effect is caused by an air spring (that is, operated by air or some other compressible fluid). If this sounds complicated it's intended to illustrate that the law relating to weight limits **is** complex.

Accurate information is required to ensure that the vehicle complies with the law and also that the driver isn't committing any offence.

The Vehicle and Operator Services Agency (VOSA – formerly the Vehicle Inspectorate and Transport Area Network) and also the police and some local authorities make spot weight checks on vehicles. Roadside checks frequently reveal contraventions of many weight limit regulations. Once identified, the police or VOSA may escort a vehicle and its driver to the nearest official weighbridge.

It's essential that all limits are complied with in order to avoid overloading, and possible prosecution.

Weight restrictions normally apply to the plated weight of a vehicle. When tractor units of articulated LGVs are being driven without a trailer they're still subject to weight limits. These relate to

- lighting regulations
- loads subject to weight limits
- lanes from which LGVs are banned on multi-lane motorways.

Regulations also include axle weight limits applying to the tractor unit, which must not be exceeded when the vehicle is loaded.

It's essential you ensure that the load is distributed correctly and safely, either on or in your vehicle. This means that loads are built up against the headboard or front wall of the body in order to reduce movement in transit. When loading your vehicle ensure that the front axle or axles aren't overloaded.

Articulated units and part-loads

To increase stability and reduce the risk of the trailer wheels lifting when turning it's preferable to have part-loads (such as an empty single ISO* container) located over the rear axle(s).

Whatever goods vehicle you drive you should study the Department for Transport publication *Code of Practice: Safety of Loads on Vehicles.*

*Note
ISO = International Standards Organisation

Recovery vehicles

Always make sure that axle loading limits aren't exceeded when a recovery vehicle removes another LGV by means of a suspended tow. This is sometimes overlooked.

Height

If you're the driver of any vehicle where the overall travelling height of the vehicle, its equipment and load (including any trailer) is more than 3 metres (10 feet) you must ensure that

- the overall travelling height is conspicuously marked in figures not less than 40 mm high in such a manner that it can be read from the driving position. It should be marked in feet and inches, or in feet and inches and in metres
- any height indicated isn't less than the overall travelling height of the vehicle.

A height notice isn't required on a particular journey if you're carrying sufficient information in documents about the route or choice of routes. This should include the height of bridges and other overhead structures to allow you to complete your journey without any risk of a collision with an overhead structure. You must then travel on the route described in these documents.

Warning devices

If a vehicle, and any trailer drawn by it, has a maximum height of more than 3 metres (10 feet) a visual warning device should warn any driver if the highest point of the equipment exceeds a predetermined height when the vehicle is being driven.

The predetermined height must not exceed the overall travelling height by more than 1 metre (3 feet 3 inches) unless the equipment has a mechanical locking device that can lock it in a stowed position. In addition, the equipment needs to be fixed in that position by the locking device when the vehicle is being driven.

The requirement for height notices, route information or warning devices won't apply if, on a particular journey you're highly unlikely to encounter any bridge or overhead structure which isn't at least 1 metre (3 feet 3 inches) higher than the maximum or overall travelling height of the vehicle.

Overhead clearances

Drivers of any vehicle exceeding 3 metres (10 feet) in height should exercise care when entering roofed premises such as

- loading bays
- depots
- dock areas
- freight terminals
- service station forecourts

- any premises that have overhanging canopies

or when negotiating

- bridges
- overhead cables
- overhead pipelines
- overhead walkways
- road tunnels
- level crossings.

Electric Cables

Overhead electricity lines crossing public roads will normally be clear for a vehicle of 5 metres (16 feet 6 inches) in height (6.1 metres (20 feet) on DfT designated high vehicle routes). As high voltage electricity can "jump" across a gap, the wire will be positioned higher than this to allow for a safe electrical clearance. This clearance **must not** be compromised.

Contact the local electricity company for advice regarding the advance notice to be given to the electricity authorities concerned (at least 19 days). You should inform them of the load, routes, etc. See your local telephone directory for details.

The power supply conductors for railways and tramways on public roads will normally allow clearance for a vehicle of 5 metres (16 feet 6 inches) in height unless the signage on the approach indicates otherwise. At level crossings where the safe height is less than 5 metres (16 feet 6 inches), a height barrier will be provided in the form of a wire supporting bells. If your vehicle will not pass under this barrier, it's not safe to pass under the electrical line.

You MUST obey the safe height warning road signs and you MUST NOT continue forward if your vehicle touches any height barrier or bells.

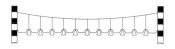

Telephone wires

If your load exceeds 5.25 metres (17 feet 6 inches) in height, the telephone companies must be notified.

Street Equipment

When planning the movement of such vehicles and loads the local Highways Authority will need to be contacted where overhead gantry traffic signs or suspended traffic lights are likely to be affected by loads over 5 metres (16 feet 6 inches).

Low Bridges

Every year around 800 incidents occur involving vehicles or their loads hitting railway or motorway bridges. An impact with any bridge can have serious consequences. An LGV, or any part of its load, colliding with a railway bridge could result in the bridge being weakened. This could also inconvenience rail traffic or create the potential for a major disaster. These factors are in addition to the costs involved in making the bridge safe, re-aligning railway tracks, and the general disruption to road and rail traffic.

The headroom under bridges in the UK is at least 5 metres (16 feet 6 inches) unless marked otherwise. Where the overhead clearance is arched this is normally **only** between the limits marked. If your vehicle collides with a bridge you must report the incident to the police. If a railway bridge is involved, report it to the railway authority as well, by calling 0845 711 4141.

Do this immediately to avoid a possible serious accident or loss of life.

Give information about

- the location
- the damage
- any bridge reference number (found on a plate bolted to the bridge or wall).

You must inform the police within 24 hours, if you don't do so at the time of the incident. Failure to notify the police is an offence.

Know your height

You **must** know the height of your vehicle and its load. Don't guess and, if in doubt, measure it. Also, don't ignore

- traffic signs
- road markings
- warning lights, bells or other audible alarms.

Don't take chances.

Height Guide	
Metres	Feet/Inches
5.0	16 6
4.8	16
4.5	15
4.2	14
3.9	13
3.6	12
3.3	11
3.0	10
2.7	9

If you aren't sure of the safe height, **stop** and call the authorities. Always

- plan your route
- slow down when approaching bridges
- know the overall vehicle/load height
- keep to the centre of arched bridges

- wait for a safe gap to proceed if there's oncoming traffic.

Width

As the driver of an LGV you must be aware of the road space that the vehicle occupies. This is particularly important where width is restricted because of parked or oncoming vehicles. Look out for signs showing restrictions.

Traffic calming measures are becoming much more common. Don't get into a situation where you're forced to reverse or turn.

Wide loads

Loads projecting over 305 mm (12 inches) beyond the width of the vehicle or those over 2.9 metres (9 feet 5 inches) but less than 3.5 metres (11 feet 5 inches) require side markers and notification to the police. Wide loads that are over 3.5 metres (11 feet 5 inches) but less than 4.3 metres (14 feet 1 inch) require side markers, police notification and an attendant. Wide loads that are 4.3 metres (14 feet 1 inch) to 5 metres (16 feet 6 inches) are also subject to the following speed limits

- 30 mph on motorways
- 25 mph on dual carriageways
- 20 mph on all other roads.

Wide loads between 5 metres (16 feet 6 inches) and 6.1 metres (20 feet) require

- side markers
- police notification
- an attendant
- Department for Transport approval

and are subject to the above speed limits.

Side marker boards must comply with regulations so that they show clearly on either side of the projection to the front and to the rear. All marker boards must be independently lit at night.

Overall Width Limits

Metres	Ft/In		
2.75	9	4	Locomotives
2.6	8	5	Refrigerated vehicles and trailers*
2.55	8	4	Motor tractors
2.55	8	4	Motor cars
2.55	8	4	Heavy motor cars
2.55	8	4	Trailers*
2.3	7	6	Other trailers

* Subject to certain conditions

Long Low Vehicles

For drivers of long low vehicles there is a risk of grounding the vehicle at some railway level crossings. A warning sign is displayed, with instructions to contact the railway controller. The vehicle must be stopped where indicated, and a phone call made to the number displayed, or by using the dedicated telephone provided. The driver must follow the instructions of the railway controller, and call back once the vehicle is safely clear of the crossing.

Large or slow vehicles

At some railway level crossings, drivers of large or slow vehicles, which might take an abnormally long time to cross the railway, must contact the railway controller before crossing. The contact with the railway controller is the same as for long low vehicles.

Length

Locations where length restrictions apply are comparatively few but they include

- road tunnels
- level crossings
- ferries
- certain areas in cities

Drivers of long rigid vehicles, either with or without drawbar trailers, or articulated LGVs must be aware of the length of their vehicle especially when

- turning left or right
- negotiating roundabouts or mini-roundabouts

- emerging from premises or exits
- overtaking
- parking, especially in lay-bys
- driving on narrow roads where there are passing places
- negotiating level crossings.

They must be particularly aware of the risk of grounding, for example on a hump bridge, which will be indicated by appropriate traffic warning signs.

Maximum Length Limits

Metres	Ft/In		
12	39	4	Rigid vehicles
16.5	54		Articulated vehicles*
18.75	61	6	Vehicle and trailer combinations**
18	59		Articulated vehicles with low-loader semi-trailer manufactured after 1 April 1991 (not including step-frame low-loaders)

Other semi-trailers			
12	39	4	Kingpin to the rear
2.04	6	7	Kingpin to any point at the front
14.04	46		Composite trailer
12	36	4	Drawbar trailer with four or more wheels, and drawing vehicle is more than 3,500 kg MGW
7	23		Other drawbar trailers

Car transporter semi-trailers

12.5	41		Kingpin to rear
4.19	13	8	Kingpin to any point at the front

* Maximum length limit for vehicles designed to carry exceptionally long indivisible loads is 27.4 metres (89 feet 9 in.).

**See *Construction and Use Regulations* (The Stationery Office) for details covering road trains.

Preventative maintenance

Ensuring that the daily walk-round checks are carried out will enable you to find any defects that could become a problem and cause the vehicle to break down or be driven whilst illegal. The time taken to complete a thorough check will be less than that required to organise repair or replacement while out on the road. Follow manufacturer's guidelines for service intervals; in addition to this, being aware of components wearing out or requiring replacement will help prevent costly breakdowns for your company,

Neglecting the maintenance of vital controls and fluids such as brakes, steering and lubricants is dangerous; they need to be checked regularly. The consequences are too great to risk driving a vehicle with defective parts.

Technical support

Traffic Commissioners and the Vehicle and Operator Services Agency (VOSA) will provide advice and assistance to operators on safety inspection intervals. VOSA offers a brake performance check service, headlight alignment and an emission check at all of its full-time heavy goods vehicle testing stations.

Daily checks

You also need to check the following regularly to ensure your vehicle is well maintained and not in need of attention. Check

- there are no fuel or oil leaks
- the security and condition of your battery
- tyres and wheel fixings
- spray suppression equipment
- steering

- excessive engine exhaust smoke
- brake hoses
- coupling security (if applicable)
- brakes.

See also the daily walk-round checks on page 77; when completed they will help you notice if any part of your vehicle needs maintenance. Always refer to the handbook for your individual vehicle before carrying out any maintenance tasks and follow any safety guidance it may contain.

Construction and functioning of the internal combustion engine

There are two main types of internal combustion engine

- spark ignition (petrol) – the fuel and air mixture is ignited by a spark
- compression ignition (diesel) – the rise in temperature and pressure during compression causes spontaneous ignition of the fuel and air mixture.

During each revolution of the crankshaft there are two strokes of the piston: the piston travels both up and down the engine cylinder. Both types of engine can be designed to operate using a two-stroke or four-stroke principle. Almost all modern goods vehicles use the four-stroke principle.

The four-stroke operating cycle

Induction stroke
The open inlet valve enables the piston to draw in a charge of air when travelling down the cylinder. With spark ignition engines the fuel is usually pre-mixed with air.

Compression stroke
Both inlet and exhaust valves close and the piston travels up the cylinder. As the piston approaches the top, ignition occurs. Compression ignition engines have the fuel injected towards the end of the compression stroke.

Expansion or power stroke

Combustion created throughout the charge raises the pressure and temperature and forces the piston down. At the end of the power stroke the exhaust valve opens.

Exhaust stroke

The exhaust valve remains open, the piston then travels up the cylinder and remaining gases will be expelled. When the valve closes, residual exhaust gases will dilute the next charge.

Diesel fuel system

Compression ignition, commonly called diesel, engines are now almost universally used for large goods vehicles and passenger carrying vehicles.

The fuel injection system functions by delivering a fine spray of a precisely controlled amount of fuel, at very high pressure and at the correct time, into the engine cylinder combustion chamber. A throttle butterfly valve, operated by the accelerator pedal, controls the amount of air delivered to the engine and the fuel quantity is adjusted to suit.

Many engines are turbocharged, where the exhaust gas drives a turbine, which compresses the incoming air and effectively delivers more air to the engine. For a given size engine the power is increased and torque is both increased and maintained over a wider engine speed range than the non-turbocharged or normally aspirated engine. Both result in improved vehicle performance.

Never use poor quality diesel fuel. This may lead to increased wear of the injection pump and early blockage of fuel injector nozzles. In winter the composition of diesel fuel is altered by the use of additives to lower the temperature at which waxing or partial solidifying of the fuel occurs. Winter grade fuels should be perfectly satisfactory in all but very severe conditions. Electrically powered fuel line heating systems are available if required.

Open the water drain valve, usually fitted to the base of the fuel filter, at least at the intervals recommended by the vehicle manufacturer.

Bleeding of fuel systems

It may become necessary to bleed the fuel system to remove any trapped air if

- the engine is new or has been renovated
- the fuel system has been cleaned or the filter changed
- the engine has not been run for a long time
- the vehicle has been driven until the fuel tank is empty.

Engine lubrication system

The engine uses a pressure-fed, full-flow, wet sump system. The oil filter, which is normally disposable, contains a bypass valve, which operates if the filter becomes blocked. A pressure relief valve controls the oil pressure; this is housed in the oil pump housing. The oil pump is driven directly from the engine.

Oil is drawn from the sump to the oil pump via a wire mesh pre-filter. The oil circulates from the pump through the main filter, which collects sediment from the oil. The oil then passes to the engine bearings and other moving parts and, having completed its circle, the oil drains back into the sump.

Always use the recommended type and viscosity of lubricant as suggested by the manufacturer. The oil should also be changed at the required recommended intervals. Friction and wear will reduce the life expectancy and the performance of a vehicle. Friction increases when there is direct metal-to-metal contact between sliding parts. Lubrication helps prevent such contact, by reducing wear from friction and heat on working parts within the engine. A film of lubrication covers the various surfaces to keep them apart and maintain fluid friction rather than dry friction.

Lubrication prevents corrosion of the internal components in the engine. It removes the heat generated in the bearings or caused by combustion and absorbed by metal components. It is also able to seal piston rings and grooves against combustion leakage.

Checking oil levels

You need to check the oil frequently: make sure the vehicle is parked on a level area not on a slope. Check the oil while the engine is cold for a more accurate result. If your vehicle is fitted with automatic transmission there may be an additional dipstick for transmission oil level checks.

You should not run the engine when the oil level is below the minimum mark on the dipstick. Don't add so much oil that the level goes above the maximum level, this creates excess pressures that could damage the engine seals and gaskets and cause oil leaks. Moving internal parts can hit the oil surface in an over-full engine causing possible damage and loss of power.

If the oil pressure warning light on your instrument panel comes on when you're driving, stop and check the oil level as soon as it is safe to do so. If the level is satisfactory, there may be a more serious problem such as failure of the oil pump, which would lead to severe engine damage.

Lubrication oil – engine

The oil in your engine has to perform several tasks at high pressures and temperatures up to 300°C. Lubrication resists wear on moving surfaces and combats the corrosive acids formed as the hydrocarbons in the fuels are burnt in the engine. Engine oil also helps to keep the engine cool. Use the lubricant recommended in the vehicle handbook.

Lubrication oil – gearbox

Most vehicles have a separate lubricating oil supply for the gearbox; it is especially formulated for gearbox use. Follow the instructions in the vehicle handbook.

Engine coolant

It is generally recognised that using an approved coolant solution containing an anti-freeze additive throughout the year will give you the best protection. Coolants ensure the cooling system will be protected from freezing in cold weather. In addition to the anti-freeze agent, coolant contains a corrosion inhibitor, which reduces oxidation and corrosion in the engine and prolongs the life of the cooling system. The anti-freeze additive is an inhibitor called ethylene glycol that has a boiling point of 195°C compared to water at 100°C. The coolant solution is usually diluted with the same volume of water to give maximum protection.

Check the coolant level frequently; if you need to top up regularly it might indicate a leak or other fault in the cooling system that will require checking. Never remove the radiator cap to refill when the engine is hot, always allow the engine to cool before adding further diluted coolant. Don't overfill the system, as the excess will be expelled as soon as the engine warms up.

Transmission system

A manual transmission system is made up of the clutch, gearbox and driveshafts. The torque is transmitted from the engine to the road wheels via the clutch and gearbox. The normal form of clutch is referred to as a friction clutch.

The clutch

This temporarily disconnects/connects the drive between the engine and gearbox. It enables the drive to be taken up gradually.

The three main components of a clutch are the drive plate, sometimes referred to as the clutch plate or friction plate, plus the pressure plate and release bearing. The drive plate is clamped between the pressure plate and the engine flywheel by spring pressure.

The engine creates the turning motion or torque, which is transmitted from the crankshaft to the flywheel. The driveshaft, attached to the friction plate, transmits the torque to the gearbox. Depressing the clutch pedal operates the release bearing to relieve the spring clamping pressure and free the drive plate.

The life of a clutch can be prolonged by careful use and avoidance of slipping or riding the clutch. Replacement should be carried out before the drive plate becomes too worn, as further use could cause the flywheel to become scored.

The gearbox

The purpose of the gearbox is to

- multiply the torque (driving force) being transmitted by the engine
- provide a means of reversing the vehicle
- provide a permanent position for neutral.

The gears contained in the gearbox allow the driver to vary the speed of the road wheels corresponding to any particular engine speed. This also results in varying the tractive effort, which is applied through the tyre to the road, to overcome the resistance to the movement of the vehicle during moving off from rest, accelerating and hill climbing.

It is common for around sixteen gear ratios to be used in the gearboxes of LGVs and PCVs and there is widespread use of semi-automatic and automatic gearbox systems to assist the driver and improve vehicle performance. In many systems there is no need for a normal clutch pedal and vehicle movement from rest is achieved in response to movement of the accelerator pedal. Gear changing may be controlled by the driver

(semi-automatic), controlled hydraulically or, increasingly, by the use of electronic systems, to change gear according to the requirements of the vehicle use situation.

The constant-mesh box is gradually being replaced with synchromesh transmission. All manufacturers now use range-changers and splitter boxes to change between the high- and low-range ratios. These use either the single-H pattern layout, (also referred to as four-over-four), or the double-H (also referred to as the four-beside-four). The gearshift layout may vary according to the make of vehicle, and you are advised to use the vehicle manual for guidance on the gear layout.

When the vehicle is cold you may have difficulty selecting a gear on a synchronised box, but once the box has had a chance to warm up, gear changing will be easier. When changing gear with a synchronised box you do not have to double declutch.

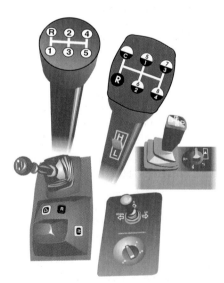

Types of gearboxes

A two speed axle is an alternative reduction gear fitted to the rear drive axle which doubles the number of available gears. The operating mechanism is fitted to the gear lever, and is electrically operated.

Splitter Box

The splitter box, like the two-speed axle, is electrically operated, but the gears are split in the gearbox rather than at the rear drive axle. Its operation is the same as the two-speed axle: a switch is fitted to the gear lever and it is possible to operate the switch and select a gear which is half a ratio higher or lower.

Range changer

The range changer is generally air operated, the gears are split in the gear box. Effectively you can change through the gears twice, once in low range, then again in the high range. Unlike the two speed axle and the splitter box, the gears may not be independently split. When reversing with this type of gear box, it must be done in the low range.

Electronic power shift

There are several similar systems, one known as EPS that uses a semi-automatic gearbox. It is simple to use, and the gear shift lever is very small with a splitter switch and a function button. The shift control is pushed forward to move forward, pulled backward for downshift and pushed left for neutral. An alarm will sound if an attempt is made to change down when engine speed is too high.

Electrical system

Much progress has been made regarding the systems within vehicles, so that most mechanical units are now controlled by electricity. The wiring requirements are so extensive in some vehicles that a system called 'multiplexing' is used. This system is computer controlled and uses a cable carrying electronic messages to switch equipment on or off. A power bus cable carries the main electric current to operate the equipment.

LGV and PCV vehicles commonly use 24 Volt lead/acid batteries to provide the power to start the vehicle. Once the engine is running, the alternator takes over and provides the electrical power needed, whilst also recharging the battery. The alternator generates electrical current and is usually directly driven by the engine via a belt. A controlled current is directed to the battery, which enables it to remain charged and provide current for other electrical systems of the vehicle, such as the lighting system.

Fuses of varying ratings, dependent on the power consumption, protect the different circuits within the vehicle. They prevent excess current from overloading the system, which may cause electrical fires. It is advisable to carry spare fuses, but make sure that you use the correct rating and find out why the fuse 'blew' before replacing it.

Care should be taken when checking batteries, as explosive gases build up and the dilute sulphuric acid used as an electrolyte will burn skin. Always follow manufacturers' recommendations when dealing with batteries.

Braking system

Applying the brakes

Planning and anticipation of road hazards should remove the need for harsh braking. Harsh or heavy braking can result in a vehicle's wheels locking, leading to a loss of vehicle control particularly on slippery road surfaces (for example, wet, icy or snow-covered).

In an emergency braking situation you may need to brake heavily. If your vehicle is equipped with an anti-lock braking system (ABS)* and you're unlikely to be able to stop the vehicle before reaching an obstruction,

Air brake system

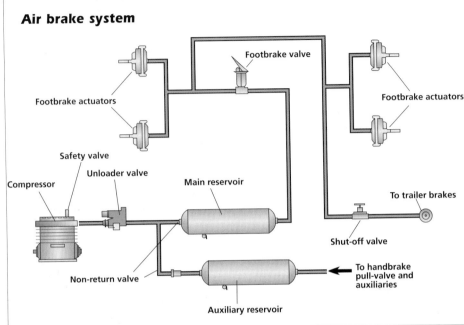

apply maximum force to the brake pedal, maintaining this force. You shouldn't 'pump' the brake pedal as this will reduce the effectiveness of the ABS system.

If your vehicle doesn't have ABS, 'wheel lock' can be controlled during heavy decelerations by 'cadence' braking, that is, rapid pumping of the brake pedal.

*Note

ABS is the registered trade mark of Bosch (Germany) for Anti Blockiersystem.

Types of brakes

There are three types of braking systems fitted to LGVs

- the service brake

- the secondary brake

- the parking brake.

The service brake is the principal braking system used and is operated by a foot control. It's used to control the speed of the

vehicle and to bring it safely to a halt. It may also incorporate an anti-lock braking system (ABS).

The secondary brake may be combined with the footbrake or the parking brake control. This brake is provided for use in the event of the service brake failing. The secondary brake normally operates on fewer wheels than the service brake and therefore has a reduced performance level.

The parking brake is usually a hand control and may also be the secondary brake. It should normally only be used when the vehicle is stationary. The parking brake must always be set when the driver leaves the driving position. It's an offence to leave any vehicle unattended without applying the brake.

LGVs are also frequently equipped with endurance braking systems (commonly called 'retarders').

Anti-lock braking systems

ABS is only a driver aid. It doesn't remove the need for good driving practices, such as anticipating events and assessing road and weather conditions. You still need to plan well ahead and brake smoothly and progressively.

Anti-lock braking systems employ wheel speed sensors to anticipate when a wheel is about to lock. Just before the wheels lock the system releases the brake and then rapidly re-applies it. This may happen many times a second to help maintain braking performance and prevent the wheels from locking. This means that you can continue to steer the vehicle during braking.

Anti-lock braking systems are in common use on LGVs, and are required by law on some. You'll need to know which vehicle combinations are required to have an ABS fitted by law. Care needs to be taken to ensure that the braking system on the tractive unit or rigid towing vehicle is compatible with the braking system on the semi-trailer or trailer.

Checking ABS

It's important to ensure that the ABS is functioning **before** setting off on a journey. Driving with a defective ABS may constitute an offence.

Modern anti-lock braking systems require electrical power for their operation. Multi-pin connectors are required to carry the electrical supply to operate the trailer brakes. The satisfactory operation of the ABS can be checked from the warning signal on the dashboard. A separate signal for the trailer is provided on the dashboard, although in some cases a signal on the trailer headboard will operate instead. The way the warning lamp operates varies between manufacturers, but with all types of signal it should be displayed when the ignition is switched on and should go out no later than when the vehicle has reached a speed of about 10 km/h (6 mph).

Endurance braking systems

Commonly referred to as 'retarders', these systems provide a way of controlling a vehicle's speed without using the wheel-mounted brakes. This can be particularly useful when descending long hills as a vehicle's speed can be stabilised without using the service brakes.

Retarders operate by applying resistance, via the transmission, to the rotation of the vehicle's driven wheels. This may be achieved by

- increased engine braking
- exhaust braking
- transmission-mounted electromagnetic or hydraulic devices.

Braking generates heat in the brakes and, at high temperatures, braking performance can be affected. The retarder leaves the service brake cool for optimum performance when required.

The system may be operated in unison with the service braking control (integrated) or by using a separate hand control (independent). Retarders normally have several stages of effectiveness depending on the braking requirement. With independent systems the driver has to select the level of performance required.

When driving on slippery surfaces care must be exercised when operating retarders if rear wheel locking is to be avoided. Some retarders are under the management of the ABS system to help avoid this problem.

Connecting a system

It's vitally important that you understand the rules which apply to connecting and disconnecting the brake lines on either an articulated vehicle or a rigid vehicle and trailer combination. You'll be asked to demonstrate this during your practical driving test.

There are two brake configurations that you may encounter – either the three-line or the two-line system. A three-line system comprises

- Emergency **red** line
- Auxiliary **blue** line
- Service **yellow** line

A two-line system has only an emergency and a service line.

Two-line vehicles and two-line trailers are obviously compatible, as are three-line vehicles and three-line trailers. A two-line motor vehicle can be connected to a three-line trailer – the trailer auxiliary line being left unconnected.

When connecting a three-line motor vehicle to a two-line trailer it's important that you follow the vehicle manufacturer's advice as to what to do with the third (blue) line. Failure to follow the manufacturer's instructions could render the combination dangerous.

When coupling a modern motor vehicle, fitted with automatic sealing valves in the 'suzie' lines, ensure that the trailer is equipped to activate them. Some older vehicles may be equipped with taps, or hand operated valves. If these are fitted you must ensure that these are opened after coupling the 'suzies' and closed before uncoupling them.

There have been a number of fatal accidents due to trailer brakes 'lifting off' as the air lines were connected. It is a mistake to believe that disconnecting the air lines engages the trailer parking brakes; on some systems it is only the emergency brake that is applied and this will release as soon as the air line is re-connected or over time as air pressure is lost from the system. Before connecting or disconnecting any brake line, ensure that the trailer parking brake has been correctly applied. This precaution **must not** be overlooked.

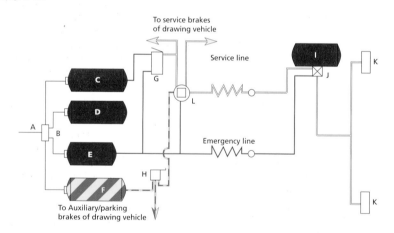

A – Supply from compressor	E – Service reservoir (trailer)	I – Trailer reservoir
B – Multi-protection valve	F – Parking/Auxiliary reservoir	J – Relay emergency valve
C – Service reservoir (front)	G – Dual foot valve	K – Single diaphragm actuators
D – Service reservoir (rear)	H – Hand control valve	L – Trailer control valve (or triple relay valve)

Example of an acceptable two-line connection: two-line vehicle drawing a two-line trailer

Safety

Air brake systems are fitted with warning devices that will be activated when air pressure drops below a predetermined level. In some circumstances there may be sufficient pressure to release the parking brake even though the warning is showing. In these cases the service brake may be ineffective. Therefore you should never release the parking brake when the brake pressure warning device is operating.

Towing vehicles are equipped with braking lines for attachment to a trailer. On modern vehicles these lines are fitted with automatic sealing valves rather then manual taps. When a trailer is coupled to a towing vehicle it's important to check that the brakes of the trailer function correctly. If they don't, remedial action must be taken **before** the vehicle is driven. Failure to do so could result in the loss of braking effectiveness on the whole combination.

Inspection and maintenance

You aren't expected to be a mechanic; however, there are braking system checks that **are** your responsibility.

Air reservoirs

Air braking systems draw their air from the atmosphere, which contains moisture. This moisture condenses in the air reservoirs and can be transmitted around a vehicle's braking system. In cold weather this can lead to ice forming in valves and pipes and may result in air pressure loss and/or system failure. Some air systems have automatic drain valves to remove this moisture, while others require daily manual draining. You should establish whether your vehicle's system reservoirs require manual draining and, if so, whose responsibility it is to make sure that it's done.

Controls

Before each journey make sure that all warning systems are working. Brake pressure warning signals may be activated automatically when the ignition is turned on (as for an ABS), or may require that you use a 'check' switch provided on the driving controls.

Never start a journey with a defective warning device or when the warning is showing. If the warning operates whilst you're travelling, stop as soon as you can do so safely and seek expert help. Driving with a warning device operating may be very dangerous and is an offence.

Tyres

All tyres on your vehicle and any trailer must be in good condition. They need to be checked weekly for damage or wear and they must be at the correct pressure. Follow manufacturers' recommendations for the correct pressure required. Neglecting tyre pressures is a major cause of tyre failure: check your tyre pressures when the tyres are cold, that is, before the vehicle is used. Ensure that all tyres are suitable for the loads being carried. Heavy goods vehicle and passenger carrying vehicle tyres have codes indicating the maximum load and speed capability. These must be suitable for the use conditions of the vehicle.

The life of a tyre will depend upon the load, inflation pressure and the speed at which the vehicle is driven. Under-inflated tyres will increase wear of the outer edge of the tread area of the tyre. Over-inflated tyres will distort the tread and increase wear in the centre of the tread area of the tyre.

Two main types of tyre construction or structure are in common use: diagonal or cross ply and radial ply. Cross ply tyres have a large number of rubber-covered textile cords which are alternately angled across the tyre from the bead, that is, the part which sits on the wheel rim, on one side to the bead on the other. This results in a rather stiff side wall, which supports the tread against steering and other side forces.

Radial ply tyres have similar textile cords, but arranged radially across the tyre almost at right angles to the width of the tread. The tyre walls are quite supple and a rubber covered steel mesh belt, which runs around the tyre underneath the tread rubber, braces the tread area. The belt keeps the tread in flat contact with the road to improve traction and grip.

Whilst both types are in use, the radial ply tyre is more favoured as it gives increased tyre life and improved safety and is more widely available in tubeless form.

For safety reasons there are very strict regulations concerning the mixing of radial and cross ply tyres on different axles. The regulations are complicated for multi-axled vehicles but for a simple single front and rear axle vehicle, radial ply tyres must not be fitted to the front axle if cross ply tyres are fitted to the rear. Tyre structures must never be mixed on the same axle.

Keeping tyres correctly inflated will help prevent failure and also improve fuel consumption: using radial ply tyres can improve consumption by 5 to 10 %.

Check wheels and tyres for balance to avoid uneven wear. When a wheel and tyre rotate they are subject to centrifugal forces. If the mass of the wheel and tyre is dispersed uniformly then the wheel is balanced. Clip on balance weights are used to rectify any imbalance.

Commercial vehicles with tubeless tyres use metal valve stems fitted to the wheel rim. Either an O-ring or a flat-flanged rubber washer makes the sealing airtight. Vehicles fitted with tube tyres have an adaptor, which is moulded to a rubber patch and vulcanised to the inner tube. The valve-stem casing is then screwed on to the tube adaptor.

Changing a tyre

Great care must be taken when changing the tyre of a large vehicle; it is often better to call out a professional tyre fitter. If you are forced to change a tyre you should

- select a firm flat surface
- check that the parking brake is applied
- ensure the passengers or other personnel are clear of the area in which you are working
- check the wheel is not damaged and that another tyre can be fitted to it
- deflate the tyre before attempting to remove the wheel
- not loosen or unscrew the clamping nuts if they are connected to divided wheel rims
- take care not to damage the flanges and locking rings when taking the tyre off.

Fitting a new tyre

Having checked the condition of the wheel before replacing with a correct sized tyre, you should

- renew the complete valve whenever a tubeless tyre is being replaced
- fit the wheel to the tyre whilst the wheel is laying flat on the ground. This will enable the tyre to fit the rim and obtain a good airtight seal
- inflate commercial tyres in a cage or similar safety cell
- inflate to 1 bar level with the valve core removed
- insert a valve core
- inflate to manufacturer's recommendation
- fully tighten wheel nuts, to the torque recommended by the vehicle manufacturer, using a calibrated torque wrench. Tighten the wheel fixings gradually and alternately diagonally across the wheel. Recheck the torque after about 30 minutes if the vehicle remains stationary or after 40 to 80 km (25 to 50 miles), if used.

Power tools are not recommended for tightening wheel fixings. It is recommended that pressure gauges are checked frequently for accuracy.

When leaving building sites or other areas with loose debris check between the tyres for bricks or other large objects that could damage your tyres or following traffic, should they fall out.

Coupling system

The coupling system, often referred to as the 'fifth wheel', is a device used to connect the tractor unit to a trailer. It permits articulation between the units. Guidance on the correct way to uncouple or recouple a unit can be found in Part Five, 'Preparing for the Driving Test' on pages 173 - 4. Follow this advice for a safe and successful completion of this procedure.

Maintenance

A fifth wheel must be maintained properly to ensure safety. It requires regular lubrication and inspection. Draw-bar units should have the eyelet checked to ensure there is no damage or wear. Heavy duty grease with a lithium or calcium base should be used for all lubrication.

Maintenance of the fifth wheel should be carried out every 10,000 km (or 1 month). To do this, uncouple the tractor and clean the fifth wheel mechanism, rubbing the plate and kingpin. Inspect the fifth wheel for damage and defects. Regrease with clean grease.

Load restraint

When securing a load you need to take into account

- the nature of the load
- the suitability of the vehicle
- the stability of the load
- the type of restraint

- protection from weather
- prevention of theft
- ease of delivery.

The object is to ensure a secure load and a stable vehicle when

- braking
- steering

even in emergency situations.

The failure of tyres on the vehicle or trailer shouldn't cause the load to become insecure. This is particularly important when stowing loads such as wooden pallets, hay, etc., which are usually stacked high on flat-bed vehicles.

Any load must be carried so that it doesn't endanger other road users at any time. It should be

- securely stowed
- within the weight limits permitted for your vehicle
- within the size limits for the vehicle (unless clearly marked or proceeding under a special movement order under escort).

You should ensure that all devices for securing the load are effective, that all

- ropes, chains and straps are secure
- sheets are fastened down
- container locking handles are secured
- doors, drop sides and tailgates are fastened
- hatches on tank vehicles are closed to prevent spillage.

You should also prevent

- material falling from bulk cement vehicles
- any nets covering skip loads being lost.

Types of load

A load may consist of large heavy pieces of machinery but that doesn't mean it will stay in place throughout a journey. Fatal accidents have occurred through such items falling from a vehicle or shifting under braking or cornering, therefore they should always be secured solidly and carefully.

When making a decision about the type of restraints to be used. consider what might happen if you have to brake hard and swerve to avoid an accident. Your vehicle might have to negotiate

- road works
- a construction site
- a lorry park

where an uneven surface may cause it to tilt over.

Material packed in plastic sacks and loaded onto pallets may be liable to slip unless 'shrink-wrapped' or secured by banding. However, material in canvas sacks may well remain totally stable.

Vehicles being carried piggy-back must always have some form of chocks applied to their wheels, in addition to a restraint. Never rely on merely a handbrake holding them in place.

Tubular loads such as scaffolding poles, lamp standards, extrusions, girders, etc. may all move forward with some force if emergency braking occurs. In such cases the headboard on the vehicle or semi-trailer can be demolished, with fatal results.

Dual-purpose trailers have been developed that incorporate a

- belly tank installed along the centre of the trailer for transporting fluids
- flat-bed deck above the tank for the conventional carriage of goods.

In such instances care must be taken not to rupture the tank below.

Safety factors relating to vehicle loads

Drivers should wear suitable personal protective equipment which employers are required to provide where there is a risk to their health and safety. This should be worn at all times where necessary during loading, carriage or delivery of goods.

Hydraulic lorry loaders and cranes have helped reduce the number of accidents that occurred during loading or unloading of the vehicles. These help drivers by reducing over-exertion and fatigue so they are better prepared to drive the vehicle.

Regulations require drivers of

- tankers carrying dangerous goods
- tanker container vehicles
- vehicles carrying dangerous goods in packages

to hold Vocational Training Certificates issued by DVLA. You must attend and pass an approved course set by the City and Guilds. They are valid for five years before needing to be renewed by attending a refresher course. These certificates must be carried when driving the relevant vehicle. It is an offence to drive a dangerous goods vehicle unless you are the holder of a valid certificate.

Further information and advice on load safety and loading equipment can be found in the Code of Practice entitled Safety of Loads on Vehicles, which is available from The Stationery Office.

Two codes of practice cover the use of lorry loaders as cranes

1. Code of Practice for Safe Use of Cranes. Lorry Loaders (BS 7121-4) – this is published by the British Standards Institute and is available from

British Standards Institute
389 Chiswick High Road
London W4 4AL

Tel: 0208 996 7474

Email: info@bsi-global.com

Website: www.bsi-global.com

and also from The Stationery Office.

2. Lorry loaders: the Code of Practice for Installation, Application and Operation – this is published by the Association of Lorry Loader Manufacturers and Importers of Great Britain (ALLMI) and is available from

Matronic Services
Peachley Court
Peachley Lane
Lower Broadheath
Worcester WR2 6QR

Tel: 01905 640 025

Fax: 01905 640 415

Types of restraint

It's important that the correct anchoring points are employed irrespective of the type of restraint being used. Remember, however, that the hooks fitted under some decks are only intended for fastening sheeting ropes.

Straps

These are generally made of webbing and are frequently used to secure many types of load.

Ensure that all straps, tensioners, etc., are kept in good, serviceable condition. If a load has sharp edges, straps with suitable sleeves and corner protectors can be used.

Battens and chocks

Large, heavy objects such as metal ingots, castings, fabrications, etc., should be chocked by nailing battens to the vehicle or trailer deck.

Chains

If there's any danger of either the weight of the load being too great for ropes or straps, or the load having sharp edges that would shear ropes or straps, then chains must be used, together with compatible tensioning devices.

53

Chains will provide added security when tree trunks or logs are being carried. Don't rely solely on vertical stanchions to hold the load.

Ropes

Traditionally, ropes have been the commonest method of securing both a load and sheets. Ropes may be of fibre or modern man-made materials, such as nylon, polypropylene, etc.

Whatever type of rope is used, you should gain experience in the correct methods of securing the load. The knots used are known in the trade as 'dolly knots'. These can only be released when required (and not otherwise). Additionally, you should ensure that the proper tension is applied and that only the correct securing points are used.

Ropes are totally unsuitable for some loads, such as steel plates, scrap metal, etc.

Sheeting

If sheeting is used – whether tarpaulin, plastic, nylon or any other material – it must be secured in such a way that it doesn't become loose and create a hazard to other road users.

When starting to cover a load with more than one sheet it's sensible to start with the rear-most sheet first, working forward. This type of overlap will reduce the possibility of wind or rain being forced under the sheeting as the vehicle travels along in bad weather conditions.

In order to secure the sheets onto a load you'll need to use the same type of knots used when restraining loads (dolly knots). These remain taut in transit but can be released with the minimum of effort.

All spare sheets and ropes must be tied down securely so that they don't fall into the path of following traffic.

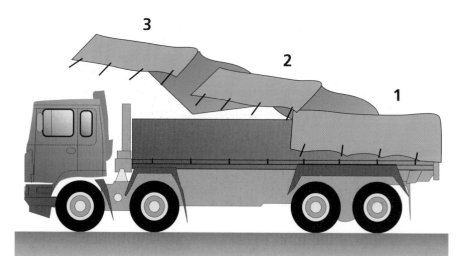

Curtain sides

The manufacturers of vehicles fitted with curtain-side bodies may be satisfied that a high degree of protection is given by the material used in their construction. This, however, doesn't relieve the driver of the responsibility for ensuring that a load is properly stowed and secured so that it won't move while in transit. This is particularly important where there may be a 'multi-drop' load of varying materials, some of which may come under the hazardous materials classification.

Take notice of warnings of poor weather conditions broadcast on the radio, especially if your vehicle is empty. Under such conditions it's often safer to secure both curtain sides at one end of the vehicle, cutting down the wind resistance and removing the likelihood of being blown over or off the road.

Container lorries

ISO (International Standards Organisation) cargo containers should only be carried on vehicles or trailers equipped with the appropriate securing points, which are designed to lock into the container body. Such vehicles may be intended for carrying

- a single 12 metre (40 feet) container
- one or two 6 metre (20 feet) containers
- larger numbers of smaller, specially designed units.

Whatever type of container is carried, all locking levers must be in the secured position during transit.

Steel ISO containers shouldn't be carried on flat-bed platform vehicles where there are no means of locking the container in position. Never rely on the weight of the container and its contents to hold it in place on a flat deck.

Ropes are totally inadequate to hold a typical seagoing steel container in place. Skeletal vehicles or trailers that have a main chassis frame with outrigger supports, into which the ISO container can be locked, are safer and more secure.

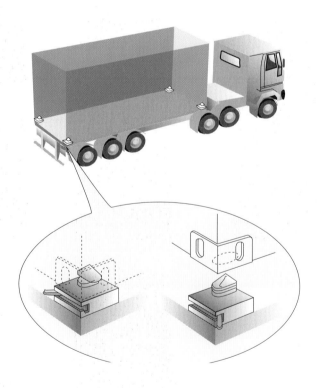

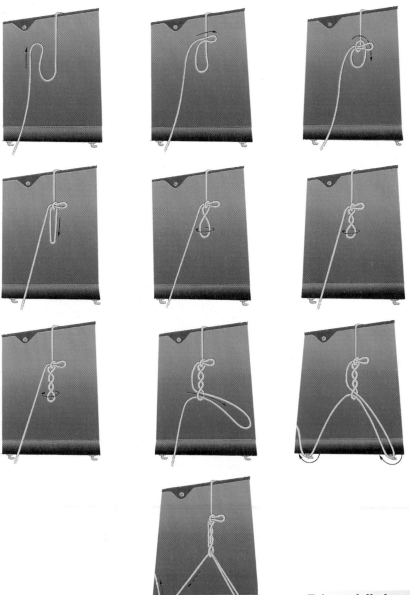

Tying a dolly knot

Part Three

Limits and regulations

The topics covered

- Environmental impact
- Drivers' hours and records
- Other regulations

Environmental impact

Transport is an essential part of modern life, but we cannot ignore its environmental consequences – local, regional and global.

There's increasing public concern for the protection of our environment, with the result that many motor vehicle manufacturers are devoting more time, effort and resources to the development of environmentally-friendly vehicles.

Considerable research and effort is taking place to develop more efficient vehicles and the following explains the effects of pollution and what you, the driver, can do to help. (You will also find further information on eco-friendly driving skills in the next chapter).

Motor vehicles account for most of the movement of people and goods.

The increased number of vehicles on the roads has damaged the environment; it has resulted in

- changes to the landscape
- air pollution, causing
  - human health problems, in particular respiratory disease
  - damage to vegetation
- building deterioration
- bridge weakening
- changes to communities
- the using up of natural resources
- disruption of wildlife.

Exhaust emissions

Fuel combustion produces carbon dioxide, a major greenhouse gas, and transport accounts for about one-fifth of the carbon dioxide we produce in this country.

MOT tests now include a strict exhaust emission test to ensure that all vehicles are operating efficiently and causing less air pollution.

Diesel engines

These engines are more fuel efficient than petrol engines. Although they produce higher levels of some pollutants (nitrogen oxides and particulates), they produce less carbon dioxide (a global warming gas). They also emit less carbon monoxide and fewer hydrocarbons.

Alternative fuels

To improve exhaust emissions even further, ultra low sulphur diesel or 'city diesel' fuels can be used. These have been formulated so that the sulphur content is very low. Sulphur is the main cause of particulates in exhaust emissions, and it also produces acid gases. The lower the content of sulphur in fuel, the less the damage to the environment.

Compressed Natural Gas (CNG)

While there are improvements in the quality of exhaust emissions produced, some of the technical disadvantages relate to the size and design of the fuel tanks required.

Electricity

Trials have been taking place with electric vehicles for a number of years, but it is only recently that advances have been made in overcoming the problems of battery size and capacity.

Fuel cells

These operate like rechargeable batteries and produce little or no pollutants, but have greater range and improved performance than most battery electric vehicles.

Hybrid vehicles

These offer the advantages of electricity without the need for large batteries. The combination of an electric motor and battery with an internal combustion engine gives increased fuel efficiency and greatly reduced emissions.

Hydrogen

This is another possible fuel source for road vehicles that is being studied. However, technical problems include storage of this highly inflammable gas.

Liquid Petroleum Gas (LPG)

This consists mainly of methane, produced during petrol refining. Vehicles can run on LPG alone or both LPG and petrol (known as 'dual fuel'). Most types of engines can be built or converted to run on LPG. Benefits include low cost, lower emissions and reduced wear and tear to engine and exhaust systems. Disadvantages include cold start problems and valve-seat wear.

Methane

Because of the naturally occurring renewable sources of this fuel, it is also being considered as a possible alternative to diesel oil, which is a finite resource.

Solar power

Needing only daylight to function, solar vehicles are small, light, slow and silent. They produce no emissions at all; however, they are very expensive as yet and improvements are needed so they can store energy for use in the dark.

Diesel spillages

Because of the extremely slippery characteristics of diesel fuel, care must be taken at all times to avoid spillages. Not only is diesel fuel dangerous to anyone stepping onto it (especially getting down from a vehicle cab), but it also creates a serious risk to other road users, especially motorcyclists.

Take care when refuelling and ensure that all filler caps and tank hatches are properly closed and secure.

Fuel consumption

Fuel consumption can depend on the design of your vehicle.

- Cab-mounted wind deflectors can effectively lower wind resistance created by large box bodies, together with lower side-panel 'skirts'.
- Tipper bodies with prominent strengthening ribs on the outside can be plated-over to give improved performance.
- A fly sheet tightly fastened over the top of tipper bodies (especially when empty) can reduce the 'drag' effect.

Further information and publications can be found on TransportEnergy's website, www.transportenergy.org.uk.

Road-friendly suspension

Reference has already been made to the requirement that some form of road-friendly suspension be fitted to vehicles which are intended to carry increased weights. By replacing springs with some form of compressible material (usually air) a reduction in vibration caused by the impact of LGV wheels on road surfaces will reduce the damage to

- the road surface itself
- adjacent structures
- under-road services (gas, water, etc.)
- bridges.

These systems can, in some instances, be fitted retrospectively to vehicles. However, this does mean that the vehicle will usually have to be equipped with additional compressed air storage tanks, creating some additional weight.

An increasing number of manufacturers are making use of the benefits that road-friendly suspension gives in reducing damage to goods in transit.

Specialised semi-trailers used to carry fragile goods have no rear axles as such. When loading takes place

- the hollow trailer body is positioned to surround the racks holding a fragile load (e.g., glass)
- the body is lowered into place
- the load is secured
- the body is raised into the travelling position.

The whole process is carried out by controlling the sophisticated road-friendly suspension system on each trailer wheel assembly.

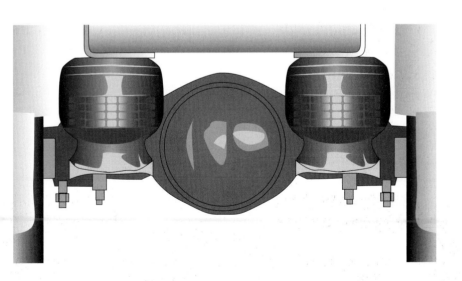

Audible warning systems

As an LGV driver it's up to you to recognise the effects your vehicle, and the way in which it's driven, can have on the environment around you.

Reversing your vehicle can cause a hazardous situation. There may be pedestrians in the area that you'll need to warn. There are different types of audible warning device which give a signal to others around the vehicle that it's reversing, such as a

- bleeper
- horn
- recorded verbal message, etc.

These must not be allowed to operate on a road subject to a 30 mph speed limit between 11.30 pm and 7 am.

Take care when setting any vehicle security alarm system. You only want such an alarm to sound when it's necessary – not by mistake.

And remember, using an audible warning device doesn't take away the need to practise good, all-round effective observation. If you think that you're unable to reverse safely you must get someone to help you.

Dangerous Goods

The Carriage of Dangerous Goods by Road Regulations 1996 (CDG Road) as amended by the Carriage of Dangerous Goods Amendments Regulations 1999 cover the rules for vehicles, operators and drivers. Explosives and radioactive materials are covered in a separate regulation.

Any quantity of dangerous goods transported in a tank or tank container must adhere to these regulations. Packaged dangerous goods rules are dependent on the transport category of the goods, the size of the containers and total load carried. Rules relate to safe parking of vehicles carrying dangerous substances: make sure you are aware of them if driving these types of vehicles.

The main requirements you should be aware of when transporting dangerous goods by road are that

- the sender of the goods must provide the vehicle operator with information in writing about the load in the form of a declaration confirming the goods are in a fit condition for carriage
- the vehicle operator must provide the driver with documents containing details about the goods prior to loading. The details must include emergency information.

These documents must be kept in the cab during transportation of the goods.

Always comply with any loading, stowing or unloading instructions. Certain dangerous goods may have to be segregated or are not permitted on the same vehicle.

Keep all vehicle marking placards that give information clean and clearly visible on your vehicle; they should be covered up or removed if no dangerous goods are being carried.

The driver of any such vehicle should ensure they have adequate training or instruction to understand the requirements associated with carrying a dangerous load.

The following groups of drivers need to be in possession of a vocational training certificate showing that they're licensed by DVLA to carry dangerous goods by road

- drivers of road tankers with a capacity of more than 1000 litres or a maximum authorised mass (MAM) of over 3.5 tonnes
- drivers of vehicles carrying tank containers, regardless of the MAM of the vehicle
- drivers of all vehicles carrying explosives (subject to limited exemptions)
- drivers of all vehicles over 3.5 tonnes MAM that are subject to the Carriage of Dangerous Goods by Road Regulations 1996.

DVLA will only issue the certificate upon receipt of proof of attending a course at an approved training establishment and passing the 7357 examination of The City and Guilds of London Institute. The certificate is valid for five years. Enquiries about courses and certificates should be directed to The City and Guilds of London Institute (see page 228 for contact details).

As well as having a vocational training certificate, the driver of a vehicle carrying dangerous goods must also have the correct driving licence entitlement for the vehicle he or she is driving.

What YOU can do to help

You have a part to play in helping to reduce the impact road transport has on the environment. You should

- plan routes to avoid busy times and congestion
- slow down. Vehicles travelling at 60 mph use more fuel to cover the same distance than those travelling at 50 mph
- anticipate well ahead
- avoid the need to 'make up time'
- cover bulky loads with sheets to reduce wind resistance
- switch off the engine when stationary in queues for a long time
- drive sensibly and always keep within the speed limit (Good driving habits save fuel.)
- use the appropriate gear and avoid over-revving in low gears
- avoid rapid acceleration or heavy braking as this leads to greater fuel consumption and more pollution. Driving smoothly can reduce fuel consumption by about 15 per cent as well as reducing wear and tear on your vehicle
- check your fuel consumption regularly
- use air conditioning sparingly – running air conditioning continuously increases fuel consumption by about 15 per cent.

Keep your vehicle well maintained

You should

- have your vehicle serviced as recommended by the manufacturer. The cost of a service may well be less than the cost of running a badly maintained vehicle. Make sure your garage includes an emissions check in the service
- make sure the engine is operating efficiently. Badly adjusted engines use more fuel and emit more exhaust fumes

- make sure filters are changed regularly
- make sure that your tyres are properly inflated. Under-inflated tyres increase fuel consumption and can be dangerous. Over-inflated tyres tend to wear unevenly and so need to be replaced more frequently
- make sure brakes are correctly adjusted
- make sure diesel injectors are operating efficiently
- if you do any of your own maintenance, make sure that you send oil, old batteries and used tyres to a garage or a local authority site for recycling or safe disposal. Don't pour oil down the drain. It's illegal, harmful to the environment and could lead to prosecution.

Select for economy and low emissions

- Vehicles with automatic transmission use about 10 per cent more fuel than similar models with manual transmission.
- Consider using ultra-low sulphur fuel, such as city diesel, as it reduces harmful emissions of particles.
- When replacing tyres, consider buying energy-saving types which have reduced rolling resistance. These increase the fuel efficiency and also improve your grip on the road.

Members of the public are encouraged to report any vehicle emitting excessive exhaust fumes.

Traffic management

Continuous research has resulted in new methods of helping the environment by easing traffic flow.

Traffic flow

The strict parking rules in major cities and towns help the traffic flow.

The Red Routes in London are an example of this and have cut journey times and improved traffic flow considerably.

Speed reduction

Traffic calming measures, including road humps and chicanes, help to keep vehicle speeds low in sensitive areas. There are also an increasing number of areas where a 20 mph speed limit is in force.

Rural area parking

Avoid parking your vehicle on the grass verge in rural areas. The weight will cause damage to the verge and often, as you drive away, mud and debris can be deposited on the road surface.

Further information on environmental issues can be found at: www.defra.gov.uk/environment/index.htm

or

ETA Services Ltd
68 High Street
Weybridge KT13 8BL

Tel: 01932 828882
Fax: 01932 829015.

Drivers' hours and records

Goods drivers' hours of work are controlled in the interests of road safety, drivers' working conditions and fair competition. A European regulation sets maximum limits on driving time and the minimum requirements for breaks and rest periods. These are known as the EC rules. Drivers who break the rules are subject to heavy fines and could lose their licence to drive LGVs. Altering drivers' hours records with intent to deceive, or tampering with tachographs, can lead to a prison sentence. Similar penalties apply to those who permit such offences. (see page 72 for new working time regulations information.)

EC rules

The EC rules apply to vehicles used for the carriage of goods, including any trailer or semi trailer, where the maximum permissible weight (MPW) exceeds 3.5 tonnes. They apply to national and international journeys throughout the European Union, and are also consistent with the rules adopted by many countries beyond. Tachographs must be used under the EC rules.

Drivers of light goods vehicles with a maximum permissible weight of 3.5 tonnes or less are not required to keep daily records but must comply with the legal limits required on maximum daily driving and daily duty time under the UK domestic drivers' hours rules.

Where a light goods vehicle of 3.5 tonnes or less (which is exempt from the EC rules due to its weight) has a trailer attached, bringing the combined weight over a maximum permissible weight of 3.5 tonnes, then EC rules will apply. Exceptions to this may arise due to the nature of the operations on which it is engaged. If none of the exemptions apply, then a tachograph must be fitted and used to monitor the hours worked under the EC rules.

Exemptions

The following are exempt from EC drivers' hours and tachograph rules. In most of these cases domestic rules apply

- vehicles used for the carriage of goods where the MPW of the vehicle, including any trailer or semi-trailer, doesn't exceed 3.5 tonnes

- vehicles with a maximum authorised speed not exceeding 30 km/h (about 18.6 mph)

- vehicles used by or under control of the armed services, civil defence, fire services and forces responsible for maintaining public order

- vehicles used in connection with the sewerage, flood protection, water, gas and electricity services, highway maintenance and control, refuse collection and disposal, telegraph and telephone services, carriage of postal articles, radio and television broadcasting, and the detection of radio or television transmitters and receivers

- vehicles used in emergencies or rescue operations

- specialised vehicles used for medical purposes

- vehicles transporting circus and fun-fair equipment

- specialised breakdown vehicles

- vehicles undergoing road tests for technical development, repair or maintenance purposes and new or rebuilt vehicles which haven't yet been put into service

- vehicles used for non-commercial carriage of goods for personal use

- vehicles used for milk collection from farms, and for the return to farms of milk containers or milk products intended for animal feed.

Drivers are also exempt from the EC drivers' hours and tachograph rules when engaged in the following transport operations in the UK. In most of these cases domestic drivers' hours rules apply

- vehicles used by agricultural, horticultural, forestry or fishery undertakings for carrying goods within a 50 km (approximately 30 miles) radius of the place where the vehicle is normally based. (In the case of fishery undertakings, the exemption applies only to the movement of fish from landing to first processing on land, and of live fish between fish farms.)
- vehicles used for carrying animal waste or carcasses that aren't intended for human consumption
- vehicles used for carrying live animals from farms to local markets and vice versa, or from markets to local slaughterhouses
- vehicles used and specially fitted for such uses as shops at local markets or for door-to-door selling; for mobile banking, exchange or saving transactions; for worship; for the lending of books, records or cassettes; for cultural events or exhibitions
- vehicles with a MPW of not more than 7.5 tonnes carrying material or equipment for the driver's use in the course of his or her work within a 50 km (approximately 30 miles) radius of the place where the vehicle is normally based, provided that driving the vehicle doesn't constitute the driver's main activity
- vehicles operating exclusively on islands not exceeding 2,300 sq km in area, which aren't linked to the rest of Great Britain by a bridge, ford or tunnel open for use by motor vehicles

- vehicles with a gross vehicle weight of not more than 7.5 tonnes (including batteries) used for the carriage of goods and propelled by means of gas or electricity
- vehicles used for driving instruction with a view to obtaining a driving licence, but excluding instruction on a journey connected with the carriage of a commercial load
- vehicles operated by the Royal National Lifeboat Institution
- vehicles manufactured before 1 January 1947
- vehicles propelled by steam
- vehicles used by health authorities, including NHS trusts, as ambulances or to carry staff, patients, medical supplies or equipment
- vehicles used by local authority Social Service departments to provide services for the elderly or the physically or mentally handicapped
- vehicles used by HM Coastguard and lighthouse services
- vehicles used by harbour or airport authorities if the vehicles remain wholly within the confines of ports or airports
- vehicles used by a train operator or any holder of a network licence which is a company wholly owned by the Crown under the Railways Act 1993, and other transport authorities when engaged in maintaining railways
- vehicles used by British Waterways Board when engaged in maintaining navigable waterways
- tractors used exclusively for agricultural and forestry work.

Tachographs

When driving within the EC rules, drivers' hours and rest periods are recorded by means of a chart that's inserted into a tachograph. A tachograph is a device that records hours of driving, other work, breaks and rest periods. It can also record the distance covered and the speed at which the vehicle travels.

The tachograph should be properly calibrated and sealed by an approved vehicle manufacturer or calibration centre. These must be checked at a Department for Transport (DfT) approved calibration centre every two years and recalibrated every six years. A plaque either on or near the tachograph will say when the checks were last carried out.

If there's anything wrong with the tachograph it should be replaced or repaired by a DfT-approved centre as soon as possible. If the vehicle can't return to base within seven days of failure of the tachograph or of the discovery of its defective operation, the repair must be carried out during the journey. While it's broken you must keep a manual record either on the charts or on a temporary chart to be attached to the charts.

Charts

You must carry enough charts with you for the whole of your journey. You'll need one for every 24 hours. You should also carry some spares with you in case the charts become dirty or damaged or if your chart is retained by an Authorised Inspecting Officer. Your employer is responsible for giving you enough clean charts of an approved type, for the tachograph installed in the vehicle.

You, the driver, must ensure that the correct information is recorded on the charts. You must enter on the chart

- your surname and first name (you should do this before departing)

- the date and the place where use of the chart begins (before departing) and ends (after arrival)

- the registration number of the vehicles driven during the use of the chart (this should be entered before departing in a different vehicle)

- the odometer reading at the start of the first journey and at the end of the last journey shown on the chart (and the readings at the time of any change of vehicle)

- the time of any change of vehicle.

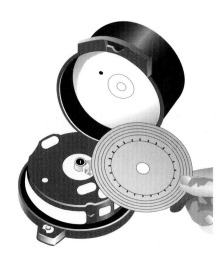

Recording information

The tachograph will start recording onto the chart as soon as it's inserted.

You must ensure that the time recorded on the chart is the official time of the vehicle's country of registration and that the mode switch is in the appropriate position. The modes are shown as symbols.

- Driving (this is automatically recorded on some tachographs)

- Other work

- On duty and available for work

- Break or rest

If you're driving more than one vehicle in one day you must take your chart with you and use it in the next vehicle. If for some reason the equipment in the other vehicle isn't compatible, you should use another chart.

If you are working away from the vehicle and cannot leave a chart in the tachograph (i.e., because the vehicle is likely to be used by someone else), or you have left a chart in but have changed work mode whilst away from the vehicle, you must make a manual entry on the reverse of the chart; i.e., OW 09.15 – 10.20

If your chart is dirty or damaged you should start another and then attach it to the damaged one.

Ensure that all the information for the day is entered on your chart(s).

The obligation to record all the complete information correctly falls on you, the driver, as well as on the operator. There are heavy fines imposed for the misuse or falsification of charts.

Chart inspections

Your tachograph records must be available for inspection by the enforcement authorities. You must carry your completed charts for the current week and the last day of the previous week on which you drove.

If your records are kept by an enforcement officer you should ask the officer to endorse the replacement chart with his or her

- name
- telephone number.

The officer should also state the number of charts retained. Alternatively, he or she may provide you with a receipt.

To ensure that all records are kept up to date and available for inspection by enforcement staff you must give the completed charts to your employer within 21 days. Employers must then retain the charts for a minimum of one year after their use and they must be submitted to enforcement officers as required.

EC drivers' hours

'Driving' means being at the controls of a vehicle for the purposes of controlling its movement, whether it's moving or stationary with the engine running.

Daily driving

A day is defined as any period of 24 hours beginning when you start other work or driving after the last daily or weekly rest period. The maximum daily hours you may drive is nine. This can be increased to 10 hours twice a week. The basic nine hours must be between

- two daily rest periods, or
- a daily rest period and a weekly rest period.

Any driving off the public roads doesn't count as driving time. In this case you should record the time as 'other work'.

You must ensure that you take a break of 45 minutes after four and a half hours of driving. This break can be replaced by two or three breaks of no less than 15 minutes during or after the driving period. The total of these shorter breaks must add up to at least 45 minutes in the four and a half hours of driving. During any break you must not drive or undertake any other work.

Daily rest periods

A rest period is an uninterrupted period time of at least one hour during which you may freely dispose of your time.

You must have a minimum of 11 consecutive hours' daily rest. This can be reduced to nine hours, but not more often than three days a week. In this case you must compensate for the reduction by taking an equivalent rest before the end of the following week.

Daily rest can alternatively be taken as 12 hours in two or three periods. In this case each rest period must be at least one hour

and the last period must be at least eight consecutive hours.

If you're taking your rest period on a ferry or train the daily rest period may be interrupted for up to one hour and includes any customs formalities, but only once. If it is, two hours must be added to the rest time. One part must be taken on land, either before or after the journey. The other part can be taken on board a boat or train. In this case you must have access to a bunk or couchette for both parts of the rest period.

Weekly driving

A week is defined as a period between 0.00 hours on Monday and 24.00 on the following Sunday.

There is no weekly driving limit, but a weekly rest period must be taken after no more than six daily driving periods. You can drive up to 56 hours between weekly rest periods, but must not exceed the limit of 90 hours in any one fortnight.

Weekly rest periods

When taking the weekly rest period, a daily rest period must normally be extended so that you get at least 45 consecutive hours of rest. You can reduce this to a minimum of 36 hours if you take the rest either where the vehicle is normally based or where you're based. If it's taken elsewhere it can be reduced to a minimum of 24 consecutive hours.

If you take reduced rest you must make up for it by taking an equal period of rest added to a weekly or daily rest period. This must be taken in one continuous period before the end of the third week following the week in question.

A weekly rest period that begins in one week and continues into the following week may be added to either of these weeks.

Catching up on reduced rest

If you've reduced your daily and/or weekly rest periods the compensatory rest must be added to another rest of at least eight hours. You can request to take this at either your base or where your vehicle is based. Rest taken as compensation for the reduction of a weekly rest period must be taken in one continuous block. Rest taken as compensation for the reduction of a daily rest period can be made up of any combination of breaks of at least one hour.

Two or more drivers

During each period of 30 hours, each driver must have a rest period of not less than eight consecutive hours. There must always be two or more drivers travelling with the vehicle for this rule to apply. A driver may take a break while another driver is driving, but not a daily rest period.

Employers must schedule work to enable drivers to comply with EC rules on drivers' hours. However, providing road safety is not jeopardised, and to ensure the safety of persons, vehicle or load, a driver may depart from the rules in order to reach a suitable stopping place. Reasons for doing so must be recorded on the back of the tachograph record sheet. This should not be a regular or repeated occurrence, as it would indicate that work was not being correctly scheduled. Planned breaches of the driver's hours are not permitted.

Domestic drivers' hours

The domestic rules apply to most goods vehicles that are exempt from EC rules.

Driving limits

You must not drive for more than 10 hours in any one day. This limit applies to the time actually spent driving. Off-road driving counts as duty rather than driving time.

Daily duty

You must not be on duty for more than 11 hours on any working day. You're exempt from the daily duty limit on any working day when you don't drive. You will also be exempt from this limit if you don't drive for more than 4 hours on each day of the week.

Exemptions

- Drivers of vehicles used by the armed forces, the police and fire brigades.
- Drivers who always drive off the public road system.
- Private driving.

Drivers of goods vehicles, including dual-purpose vehicles or those not exceeding 3.5 tonnes MPW, are exempt from the duty limit, but not the driving limit where they are used by

- doctors
- dentists
- nurses
- midwives
- vets.

Vehicles used for any inspection, cleaning, maintenance, repair, installation or fitting

- by a commercial traveller
- by the AA, RAC or RSAC
- for cinematograph or radio and television broadcasting

are included among the exemptions.

The domestic rules also allow for events needing immediate action to avoid danger to life or health of people or animals, and for the prevention of serious disruption to essential services or for danger to property.

Keeping records

You must keep a written record of your hours of work on a weekly record sheet, which is available from commercial printers. If you're driving a vehicle in excess of 3.5 tonnes MPW that carries parcels on postal services you must use a tachograph.

Mixed EC and domestic driving

It's possible that you may drive under EC rules and domestic rules during a week or even one day. You can choose to drive under EC rules for the whole of the time. If you use a combination of both sets of rules you must ensure that EC limits are not exceeded when driving vehicles on EC work.

You can't use the time driving under EC rules as off-duty time under the domestic rules; driving under EC rules counts towards the driving and duty limits under the domestic rules. Similarly, you can't claim driving and other work under domestic rules as rest time for EC rules. Remember, any EC driving in a week means that you must take daily and weekly rest periods.

Other regulations
Rules on Working Time

Drivers subject to the UK domestic drivers' hours rules are affected by four provisions under the Horizontal Amending Directive (HAD), introduced on 1 August 2003. These are:

- a requirement to limit hours to no more than an average 48 hour week (although individuals will be allowed to "opt-out" of this requirement, if they want to)
- an entitlement to 4 weeks paid annual leave
- health checks for night workers
- an entitlement for adequate rest.

The reference period for calculating the 48 hour average working week is normally a rolling 17 week period. However, this reference period can be extended up to 52 weeks, if representatives from both sides of industry can agree to do so. Self-employed drivers are not subject to the HAD, but they may be affected by the road transport directive in 2009.

Drivers subject to EU drivers' hours and tachograph rules are required to adhere to separate working time provisions under the Road Transport (Working Time) Regulations, which came into force in March 2005. The following are the main provisions of UK's implementing regulations:

Weekly 'Working time': must not exceed an average of 48 hours per week (calculated over the reference period of 17 weeks). A maximum working time of 60 hours can be performed in any single week, providing the average 48 hour limit is not exceeded.

Night Work: will be limited to 10 hours working time in a 24 hour period, where any work is carried out during the night time period 00.00 - 04.00hrs. The 10 hour limit may be exceeded if this is permitted under a collective or workforce agreement.

Breaks: When driving is being carried out, the break provisions under EU drivers' hours rules (EC/3820/85) take precedence. However, drivers are not permitted to work for more than 6 consecutive hours without a break. Where working hours total between 6 & 9 hours a day, a break of at least 30 minutes is required. A further 15 minute break is required (45 minutes in total) if total working hours exceed 9 hours. Break periods can be divided, but their duration must be at least 15 minutes long.

Rest: Same as EU or AETR drivers' hours rules (EC/3820/85).

Record keeping: Records need to be kept for 2 years after the period in question.

As stated previously, the reference period for calculating the 48 hour week is normally 17 weeks, but it can be extended to 26 weeks if this is permitted under a collective or workforce agreement. There is no "opt-out" for individuals wishing to work longer than an average 48 hour week, but break periods and 'periods of availability' will not count as working time.

Examples of what might count as a period of availability are: accompanying a vehicle on a ferry crossing or waiting while other workers load/unload your vehicle (waiting time may only be classed as availability, if the duration of any such periods are known about in advance by the driver). For mobile workers driving in a team, a period of availability also includes time spent sitting next to the driver while the vehicle is in motion.

Goods vehicle operator licensing

Users of most commercial goods vehicles weighing over 3.5 tonnes must have a goods vehicle operator's licence. This applies even if they use a hired vehicle or only use the vehicle for one day. The licence authorises an operator to use a maximum total number of motor vehicles and trailers and a specific operating centre or centres where the vehicles are normally kept when not in use.

There are three types of licence

* Restricted, which allows an operator to carry his/her own goods in connection with his/her business

* Standard National, which allows an operator to carry his/her own goods and goods for other people for hire or reward in Great Britain

* Standard International, which allows an operator to carry his/her own goods and goods for other people for hire or reward, both in Great Britain and on international journeys.

Licence applications are made to statutorily independent Traffic Commissioners, who are appointed by the Secretary of State for Transport. Great Britain is divided into six Traffic Areas (for contact details of the Traffic Area Offices, see pages 226 and 227). An operator must hold a licence in each Traffic Area where an operating centre or centres exist. A free guide for operators summarising the legislation is available from Traffic Area Offices.

If you wish to appeal against a Traffic Commissioner's decision or require further details of the appeals procedure, a free booklet can be obtained from
The Transport Tribunal
48-49 Chancery Lane
London WC2A 1JR
Tel: 020 7947 7493.

The booklet is also available from your local Traffic Area Office.

Northern Ireland operations

Northern Ireland has a separate system administered in the Province by the Road Transport Licensing Division of Driver and Vehicle Licensing Northern Ireland (DVLNI). It is not necessary for operators in the Province to obtain a short term 'O' licence before entering Great Britain. Holders of current 'O' licences or Northern Ireland Road Freight Operator Licences are permitted to carry goods in each country.

Documentation

Driving in Europe

When driving in Europe you must carry your national driving licence, insurance certificate and vehicle registration document. Other documentation may also be required for some countries.

International carriage of goods by road

Any goods being carried for hire or reward on international journeys under the provision of the Convention on the Contract for the International Carriage of Goods by Road (CMR) must be recorded on CMR consignment notes. These consignment notes confirm that carriage is being undertaken in agreement with the CMR Convention. There are four copies: the consignor keeps one copy, one copy goes to the consignee, the third copy must travel with the vehicle and the remaining copy is kept on file by the originator.

Where it is necessary to divide the consignment then separate consignment notes can be made for the individual parts of the consignment.

Consignment notes for own-account carriage by road

Own-account operators are not required to use CMR consignment notes for international journeys. Any journey that can be shown as on own account, not for hire or reward, need only have a simple consignment note.

Customs procedures and documentation

Since 1993 goods being shipped to EU countries are no longer classified as exports. They are known as despatches as long as they are of EU origin and in free circulation within the EU. They are classed as having Community status, can be transported between EU member states and are no longer subject to Customs procedures. These goods require an invoice, a transport document or a completed copy 4 of the Single Administration Document (SAD).

Customs requirements for exports outside the EU

A declaration of entry must be made to Customs and Excise if exporting to non-EU countries (with certain exceptions).

The driver's responsibility for the receipt, carriage and delivery of goods

The driver is responsible for the contents of their vehicle and needs to ensure that it is loaded correctly for stability and ease of access. The goods should be delivered to the appropriate persons at the agreed time within the deadlines set. Always allow sufficient time to get to the individual premises but do not allow a deadline to make you exceed the speed limits for the areas or conditions.

The goods should arrive in the condition they were in when collected or loaded onto the vehicle. Do not let lack of attention cause damage to the goods during loading or unloading. The goods should be delivered in accordance with any agreed conditions set for that contract.

Ensure any paperwork has the required signatures for handover of the goods. Retain the required paperwork to enable work records to be maintained.

Know the regulations

In addition to the rules and regulations that apply to drivers' hours, vehicles and loads, you should be sure that you comply with any regulations which affect your

* health
* conduct
* vehicle
* driving
* licence
* safety.

It's essential that you know and keep up to date with the regulations and the latest official advice.

Your health and conduct

Health

Even apparently simple illnesses can affect your reactions. You should be on your guard against the effects of

* flu symptoms
* hay fever
* a common cold
* tiredness.

Falling asleep

Incidents where vehicles have

* left the road
* collided with broken-down vehicles, police patrols and other persons on the hard shoulder of motorways

have been attributed to falling asleep at the wheel. The introduction of

* air-suspension drivers' seats
* 'floating' cab suspension
* air suspension on vehicles
* quieter, smoother diesel engines
* more widely adopted sound-proofing materials

has produced a comfortable 'cocoon' environment where you'll spend most of your working day. This can easily cause tiredness.

Seat belts

From 1 March 2005, changes in seat belt laws mean it is compulsory for drivers and passengers, in vehicles constructed or adapted to carry goods, to wear their seat belts while making deliveries or collections when travelling over 50 metres.

Be on your guard against boredom on comparatively empty roads or motorways, especially at night. Always

- take planned rest stops
- keep a plentiful supply of fresh air circulating in the cab
- avoid allowing the cab to become unduly warm
- avoid driving if you aren't 100 per cent fit to drive
- avoid driving after a heavy meal.

Stop at the next lay-by or pull off the motorway (or slip road) if you start to feel tired.

Drugs

Drug abuse has now reached the point where well-known multinational companies have introduced random drug-testing for their drivers. Those drivers who fail such tests may face instant dismissal.

It should be obvious that you must not take any of the drugs that are generally accepted as 'banned substances' whilst driving. These include

- amphetamines (e.g. 'diet pills')
- methylamphetamines (MDMA)
- benzodiazepine (tranquillizers)
- methaqualone (sleeping pills)
- barbiturates (sleeping pills)
- propoxyphane
- phencyclidine ('Angel Dust')
- cannabis
- cocaine
- heroin
- morphine/codeine.

Unlike alcohol (the effects of which last for about 24 hours) many of the effects of drugs will remain in the system for up to 72 hours.

Off-the-shelf remedies Even everyday cold or flu remedies can cause drowsiness. Read the labels carefully. If in doubt, consult either your doctor or pharmacist. If still in doubt, **don't drive**.

Alcohol

It's an offence to drive with more than

- a breath alcohol level in excess of 35 μg per 100 ml
- a blood alcohol level in excess of 80 mg per 100 ml.

Don't drink if you're going to drive

Be aware that alcohol may remain in the body for around 24 hours. The effects on your reactions will be evident the next morning, and you could fail a breath test.

If you're convicted of a drink–driving offence while driving an ordinary motor vehicle, a driving ban will result in you losing your LGV entitlement and your livelihood.

Your vehicle

The law relating to vehicles is extensive. Manufacturers, operators and drivers all must obey specific regulations.

The manufacturer is responsible for ensuring that the vehicle is built to comply with the Construction and Use Regulations.

The operator is responsible for making sure that a vehicle

- continues to comply with those regulations
- meets all current requirements and new regulations as they're introduced
- is tested as required
- displays all required markings, discs and certificates
- is in a serviceable condition, including equipment, fittings and fixtures.

In addition, the operator must operate a system whereby drivers of the vehicle can report defects and have them solved effectively. The operator shouldn't cause or permit a vehicle to be operated in any way other than the law allows.

Daily walk-round check

A daily walk-round check should be carried out by the driver. The driver has a legal responsibility for

- taking all reasonable precautions to ensure that legal requirements are met before driving any vehicle
- checking that the vehicle is fully roadworthy and free from significant defects before driving it
- ensuring that any equipment, fittings or fixtures required are present and serviceable

- not driving the vehicle if any fault develops that would make it illegal to be driven
- ensuring that all actions taken whilst in charge of the vehicle are lawful.

You should consider whether it would be illegal to drive the vehicle if anything that should by law be fitted to or carried on the vehicle isn't in place or in a serviceable condition.

The daily walk-round check should cover

- brakes
- lights
- tyres
- windscreen wipers and washers
- horn
- mirrors
- speedometer
- tachograph
- number plates
- reflectors and reflective plates
- exhaust system
- any coupling gear
- speed limiter
- correct plating
- current test certificate (if required)
- proper licensing with the appropriate valid disc(s) displayed
- insurance
- seat belts*
- construction and use
- any load being carried.

Note
Where seat belts are fitted they must be worn.

You should consider the legal status if something is fitted to the vehicle which isn't required by law but is

- unserviceable
- in a dangerous condition
- not fitted so as to comply with the regulations.

For example, your vehicle isn't required by law to have spot or front fog lights. However, if they're fitted, they must be positioned no less than 0.6 m (2 feet) from the ground.

'Red' diesel fuel is restricted to use for authorised purposes only. Any driver whose vehicle is found to be illegally operating on this fuel will face severe penalties for attempting to evade excise duty. Roadside checks are frequently carried out by HM Customs and Excise officers.

The Vehicle and Operator Services Agency (VOSA) and police carry out frequent spot checks of vehicle condition. Where serious defects are found, the vehicle is prohibited from further use until the defects are rectified, and details of the prohibition are notified to the Traffic Commissioner.

Cockpit drill

Make these checks for the safety of yourself, any passengers and other road users.

Every time you get into your vehicle, check that

- the driving seat is correctly adjusted, so that you can sit with a correct posture, reach all controls comfortably and take effective observations
- all interior and exterior mirrors are clean and correctly adjusted
- lenses and screens of rear-view video equipment are clean and clear
- gauges and warning systems are working correctly (never start a journey with a defective warning device or when a warning light is showing)
- the parking brake is applied
- the gear selector is in neutral (or in 'Park' if driving an automatic vehicle)
- you have sufficient fuel for your journey or until you can next refuel
- your mobile phone is switched off
- the doors are working correctly and are closed before moving off.

Before starting your journey, make sure you know and understand the

- controls: where they are and how they work

- vehicle size: its width and height, and its weight
- handling: the vehicle's characteristics
- brakes: whether ABS brakes are fitted.

Road speed limiters

Vehicles which require speed limiters

- A goods vehicle with a maximum gross weight in excess of 7,500 kg but not exceeding 12,000 kg, which was first used on or after 1 August 1992, and would, if a speed limiter were not fitted, have a relevant speed exceeding 60 mph.
- A goods vehicle with a maximum gross weight in excess of 12,000 kg, which was first used on or after 1 January 1988, and would, if a speed limiter were not fitted, have a relevant speed exceeding 56 mph.

Exemptions Speed limiter requirements don't apply to a vehicle that's

- being taken to a place where a speed limiter is to be installed, calibrated, repaired or replaced
- completing a journey in the course of which the speed limiter has accidentally ceased to function
- used for police, fire or ambulance purposes
- used for naval, military or air force purposes when used by the Crown or owned by the MOD
- being used no more than six miles on a public road in any calendar week between land occupied by the vehicle keeper.

Types

There are two main types of speed limiters. One type works by the mechanical or electrical actuator, the other works through the vehicle's engine management system.

Principles of operation

The speed limiter works by receiving a road speed signal either from the tachograph or a sensor fitted to another system on the vehicle, such as the Anti-Lock Braking System (ABS). Occasionally a specific sensor for the speed limiter system may be fitted. The vast majority of vehicles are fitted with speed limiters that take the speed signal from the tachograph.

Irrespective of the type of sensor used, the information is transmitted to the Electronic Control Unit (ECU) which, in turn, controls the equipment used to regulate the power output or revolutions of the vehicle's engine. This is normally achieved by reducing the amount of fuel supplied to the engine.

Parts

The system will consist of a road speed sensor (this may or may not be part of the tachograph system), an electronic cable, an Electronic Control Unit (this may or may not be part of the vehicle's engine management system), an actuation device (this may be a pump, relay or valve) and a plate that is fitted to the vehicle to show the set speed.

Connections

Authorised speed limiter centres can only carry out installation, repairs and calibration. These centres will seal all connections between the speed sensor, Electronic Control Unit and the actuation device to ensure the system is tamper-proof.

Maintenance

There is no day-to-day maintenance required, although any failure of the road speed limiter must be reported to the operator of the vehicle, who should arrange for the repair at the end of the journey upon which the vehicle is engaged.

Your driving

You must drive at all times within the law and comply with

- speed limits
- weight limits
- loading/unloading restrictions
- waiting restrictions
- stopping restrictions (clearways)
- lighting regulations
- restrictions of access to
  - pedestrian precincts
  - residential areas
  - traffic calming zones
  - play streets
- all traffic signs
- road markings
- traffic signals at
  - junctions
  - level crossings
  - fire or ambulance stations
  - lifting or swing bridges

- signals given by authorised persons
  - police officers
  - traffic wardens
  - Highways Agency Traffic Officers
  - Vehicle & Operator Services Agency officers
  - local authority parking attendants
  - school crossing patrols
  - persons engaged in road repairs
- motorway regulations
- regulations governing specific locations
  - tunnels
  - bridges
  - ferries
- pedestrian crossing rules.

Driving licences

The LGV driving licence is a necessity if you wish to earn your living driving large goods vehicles. It's essential that when you drive any vehicle other than an LGV your driving continues to be up to the highest standards. If you accumulate penalty points on your category B licence, eventually your LGV licence will be at risk.

Speed limits

Your vehicle may be fitted with a speed limiter, which will generally prevent you from exceeding motorway speed limits. However, it won't stop you exceeding lower speed limits. Observing speed limits is part of your responsibility. The speed limits that apply to different classes of vehicles on different types of roads are found in *The Highway Code*.

Speeding offences

Police forces and local authorities are now using the most up-to-date technology in an effort to persuade drivers to comply with speed limits.

At some locations fixed cameras that photograph vehicles exceeding the speed limit have been installed. Improved detection equipment can now also 'lock on' to individual vehicles in busy traffic flows.

In addition, new electronic systems now display the registration number and speed of any offending vehicle at selected motorway locations with a view to 'showing up' the driver concerned.

Drivers whose speed is considerably higher than the legal speed limit can expect a proportionately higher penalty if a successful prosecution results. But remember, the aim is to improve driving standards, not to increase prosecutions.

Red light cameras

Cameras have been installed at many notorious accident spots to record drivers not complying with the traffic signals. These are also intended to act as a deterrent and to improve safety for road users in general.

Whether it relates to an alleged speeding or traffic signal offence, any photograph produced as evidence and that shows the

- time
- date
- speed
- vehicle registration number
- time a red signal had already been showing

will prove difficult to dispute.

Red Routes

On many roads in London yellow lines have been replaced with red lines. A network of priority (Red) routes for London was approved by Parliament in June 1992 as a means of addressing traffic congestion problems and widespread disregard of parking restrictions in the capital. Red Route measures currently apply to 580 miles of London's roads.

Yellow-line exemptions **don't** apply on Red Routes. During the day loading is only allowed in marked boxes. Overnight and on Sundays most controls are relaxed to allow unrestricted stopping. It's important to check signs carefully as the hours of operation for Red Routes vary from area to area.

Red Route controls are enforced by Metropolitan Police traffic wardens.

There's a fixed fine for illegal stopping on a Red Route, with no discounts for early payment.

The police or traffic wardens are able to provide limited dispensations for the rare occasions when loading provisions are not adequate. These will be available from the local police station.

There are five main types of Red Route markings. The graphic below shows the layout of various lines on the road. You will find all the signs more clearly laid out, along with their respective lines, on page 137.

Double red lines   These ban all stopping 24 hours a day, seven days a week. You aren't allowed to stop for

*   loading
*   dropping off passengers
*   visiting shops.

Single red lines   These ban all stopping during the daytime, such as 7 am to 7 pm Monday to Saturday. Outside these hours unrestricted stopping is allowed.

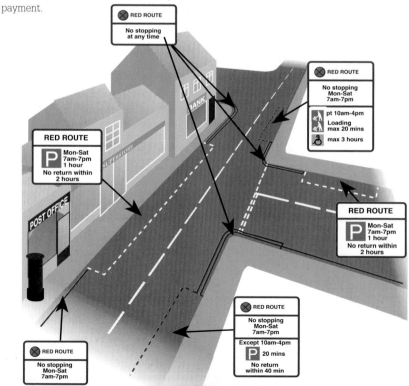

Parking boxes allow vehicles free short term parking and can be used for loading.

- *Red* - allow parking or loading outside rush hours, eg 10 am to 4 pm, for periods of 20 minutes to one hour.
- *White* - allow parking or loading at **any** time, but a stay may be restricted to 20 minutes or an hour during the day.

At other times, such as 7 pm to 7 am and on Sundays, unrestricted stopping is allowed in either type of parking box.

Loading boxes mark the areas where only loading is allowed. 'Loading' is when a vehicle stops briefly to load or unload bulky or heavy goods. These goods must be heavy or bulky enough so that it isn't easy to carry them any distance and it may involve more than one trip. If this is not the case, then your vehicle should be parked legally and the goods carried to the premises. Picking up portable items, like shopping, doesn't constitute loading.

- *Red* - allow loading outside rush hours, eg 10 am to 4 pm, for a maximum 20 minutes.
- *White* - allow loading at **any** time, but during the day, a stay is restricted to a maximum of 20 minutes.

At other times, such as between 7 pm and 7 am and on Sundays, unrestricted stopping is allowed in either type of loading box.

Clearways are major roads where there's no need to stop. There won't be red lines but Red Route clearway signs will indicate that stopping isn't allowed at any time.

Further red route information can be found in chapter four, and you can also contact

Transport for London Street Management
Windsor House
50 Victoria Street
London SW1H 0TL

Tel: 020 7941 4500

Congestion charging

A congestion charging scheme is operational in central London to help reduce traffic and make journeys and delivery times more reliable. The congestion charge applies from 7.00 am to 6.30 pm Monday to Friday, excluding public holidays. Failure to pay the charge will lead to a fine.

Exemptions   Those who are exempt from the charge include

- disabled drivers
- residents who live within the congestion charging zone
- alternative fuel vehicles
- vehicles with nine or more seats
- roadside recovery vehicles
- all two-wheeled vehicles
- London licensed taxis and minicabs.

Drivers in some categories of exemption need to register with Transport for London (see congestion charging contact details below).

Discounts   Businesses and other organisations operating a fleet of 25 or more vehicles are entitled to a discount when they register with a dedicated fleet scheme.

For more information, to register or to make a payment, ring the Congestion Charge Line, tel. 0870 900 1234 or visit the website www.cclondon.com.

Congestion charging is also in operation in Durham and may be introduced in other towns.

Health and safety

Many more activities have become the subject of Health and Safety regulations. These include

- limits to the weight of objects that should be lifted manually, e.g. loading packages
- provision of protective clothing
  - reflective jackets
  - boots
  - gloves
  - warm clothing
  - hard hats

where appropriate to the nature of the work.

Asbestos

During vehicle maintenance, drivers should be aware of the dangers to health from asbestos dust especially when dealing with components known to contain this material, such as

- brake shoes
- clutch plates
- tank or pipe lagging.

Safe working practice

Extra care must be taken when working

- near or over inspection pits (danger of falling)
- under hydraulically raised tipper bodies (danger of being crushed – use props)
- near engines emitting exhaust fumes (breathing problems)
- with solvents or degreasing agents (lung and skin problems)
- close to vehicle batteries (risk of burns or explosion)
- at the rear of a vehicle fitted with a 'tail-lift' mechanism (foot injuries)
- in or near paint spray shops (lung problems from vapour).

Anti-theft measures

Instances of theft of vehicles and trailers are unfortunately common. You're responsible for your vehicle, so you should reduce the risk of it being stolen.

- Don't discuss details of your load with any unauthorised person.
- Never leave the keys in the cab while it's unattended, even if you're at the rear of the vehicle.
- You can't afford to give a lift to anyone, however plausible their story or innocent they look.
- Wherever possible, try to avoid using the same route and making the same drops and rest stops.
- Have all major components (plus glass) security etched with the vehicle identification number (VIN).
- Only park in secure, well-lit, reputable overnight lorry parks if your rest stops can be planned this way.
- One simple but effective measure that many drivers adopt at overnight stops is to park with the rear doors of their vehicle or its trailer/container hard up against another vehicle. This works well on most occasions.
- Keep your mobile telephone handset with you, if one is available.
- Avoid parking in obviously vulnerable areas if at all possible.
- Ensure that all doors are locked and the windows secure if you sleep in the cab overnight.
- Always ask to see the identity of any officer who might stop you.
- Have an alarm system and/or immobiliser fitted to the vehicle by a reputable security specialist, and approved by the insurance company.

- Avoid leaving any trailer unattended unless on approved secure premises.
- Fit a kingpin or drawbar lock to any trailer that has to be left unattended. Operators are advised to seek the advice of the local crime prevention officer, especially if engaged in the transit of high-value merchandise.

Large numbers of LGVs are stolen in Britain every year. Most of these vehicles are never recovered. Stay vigilant; if you see anything suspicious, ring 999 and report it.

Part Four

Driver skills

The topics covered

- Professional driving
- Driving at night
- Motorway driving
- All-weather driving
- Avoiding and dealing with congestion
- Green Issues - helping the environment
- Accidents
- First Aid
- Breakdowns

Professional driving

Essential skills

A professional driver should develop the skills necessary to make clear, positive decisions about situations encountered on the road. The following are the skills you'll require.

Control

You should develop the physical skills that enable you to be in control of your vehicle at all times. You should know how your vehicle and its load will handle in any situation you encounter by understanding its capabilities and limitations.

Awareness

You need to know what's happening around you so that you're always conscious of any potential hazards that might develop. This will give you the time to deal with them as they occur.

Planning

Proper planning means that you'll be able to act early when approaching junctions or hazards. This will prevent unnecessary braking and gear-changing, helping you to make progress in traffic. Loaded large vehicles take longer to gain speed than smaller vehicles. Other road users will appreciate your ability to avoid late signalling, constant braking and slow acceleration away from hazards.

Anticipation

By knowing the correct way of dealing with situations as they occur you'll develop anticipation of how to behave in those instances. You'll also have a better insight into the way others respond to those same situations.

It's essential that you're in control of your vehicle at all times. You should drive skilfully and plan ahead so that your vehicle is travelling at the appropriate speed and in the correct position for the next manoeuvre you need to take. You should never have to rush or take action hastily. By adopting the correct techniques you'll create the time and room to complete your intentions safely.

Other road users

Others on the road might make mistakes. You have to accept that other road users aren't always aware of the extra room or time you need, due to the size of your vehicle.

Young children

Young children are particularly unpredictable and might run out into the road suddenly. If you're passing pedestrians who are walking on the pavement but close to the kerb, you must be aware that the size of your vehicle could cause a draught. This could unsteady a small child or, indeed, an adult. Always check your nearside mirror as you pass.

The elderly

Some elderly pedestrians may have poor eyesight or hearing difficulties. This might make them indecisive and they may sometimes become confused. They also might take longer to cross the road. You need to understand this and allow them more time.

Elderly drivers might be hesitant or become confused at major junctions or gyratory systems. Don't intimidate them by driving up too close or revving the engine.

Learner drivers

Learner drivers who aren't used to all driving situations and other types of road user might be affected by a close-following LGV. They might be driving at an excessively slow speed or be hesitant. Be patient and give them room.

Cyclists

In 2001, over a quarter of cyclist fatalities in road traffic accidents resulted from a collision with an LGV*, yet goods vehicles comprised only about seven per cent of the traffic on UK roads.

You need to allow cyclists as much room as you would a car. They might swerve to avoid a drain cover or a steep camber in the road. If they're approaching a junction or roundabout, you must be aware that they might turn right from the left-hand lane, crossing the path of traffic.

The size and shape of your vehicle makes it essential that you're aware of the presence of cyclists **all around** you. Use your nearside mirror as you pass a cyclist to ensure that you've done so safely.

Be aware when you're waiting at a junction that they might move up along either side. If they're positioned in front of your nearside mirror, between the kerb and your front nearside wheel, they'll be difficult to see. You should be aware of this situation as it develops and allow them to move away before you move off.

If you see a cyclist ahead of you glancing round to their right, they're probably about to turn right. Allow for this.

*Note

These figures are taken from Road Accidents Great Britain: 2001, The Casualty Report, which is published by the Stationery Office for the Department for Transport.

Horses and other animals

Horses are easily frightened by

- noise
- headlights or flashing lights
- vehicles passing too close.

If you see horse riders ahead, either on the road or on the grass verge, plan your approach carefully. Slow down safely and don't rev the engine. You should allow for the fact that some of the riders might be learners and may not have full control if the animal is startled or frightened. Novice riders may sometimes be on a leading rein and have someone walking with them.

When you pass them, do so slowly and leave plenty of room.

Always check your nearside mirror to ensure that you've safely completed the manoeuvre. Don't flash your headlights unnecessarily, and DO NOT release air brakes behind animals, particularly horses as this could cause them to shy or bolt.

Effective observation

Due to the height of the cab you may have a better view from your driving position than other road users. You can take advantage of this, for example, when approaching a blind bend, by using your added height to see over hedgerows or other obstructions; you can then scan ahead for potential hazards. However, because of its size and design an LGV will have more blind spots than many smaller vehicles.

You should use the mirrors constantly and act upon what you see in them to assess what road users around you are doing or might do next. You must frequently check down the sides of your vehicle.

Check the offside

- for overtaking traffic coming up behind or already alongside. Do this before signalling
- before changing lanes, overtaking, turning right or moving to the right.

Check the nearside

- for cyclists or motorcyclists 'filtering' up the nearside
- for traffic on your left when moving in two or more lanes
- when you've passed another road user, pedestrians or parked vehicle before moving back to the left
- to verify the position of the rear wheels of your vehicle or trailer in relation to the kerb
- before changing lanes, after overtaking, turning left or moving closer to the left when leaving roundabouts.

You should use your mirrors frequently so that you're constantly aware of what's happening around you.

Because of your relatively high seating position you should check for pedestrians or cyclists who may be directly in front of the vehicle but out of your normal field of vision, especially

- at pedestrian crossings
- in slow-moving congested traffic.

Remember, just a simple glance isn't enough. You need to check carefully.

Some LGVs, particularly those with sleeper cabs, give very limited vision to the side. When moving away, wind down the window and lean out and look round to ensure that it's clear **before** the vehicle starts to move.

Many modern vehicles are fitted with an additional nearside mirror specifically positioned so that the driver can observe the nearside front wheel in relation to the kerb. Use it whenever you're moving off or pulling in to park alongside the kerb, and to check the vehicle's position when you have to move close to the left in normal driving.

Striking the kerb at speed or wandering onto a verge can seriously deflect the steering or damage the tyre.

Mirrors

When you're learning to drive, get into a routine of checking your mirrors. It's important to know as much about traffic conditions all around you as it is about what's going on ahead.

Before you consider changing direction or altering speed you should assess how your actions will affect other road users. Most non-LGV traffic attempting to overtake will normally be catching up to your vehicle at noticeably higher speeds.

You should use the mirrors well before you signal your intention or make any manoeuvre, such as

- moving away
- changing direction
- turning left or right
- overtaking
- changing lanes
- slowing or stopping
- speeding up
- opening the cab door.

Your mirrors should be

- clean and free from dust and grime
- properly adjusted to give a clear view behind. This is particularly important when you're transporting an oversized load that projects over the normal width of the vehicle.

Looking isn't enough

You must act sensibly and positively on what you see. Take note of the speed, behaviour and likely intentions of following traffic.

Take care not to allow your vehicle to 'wander,' however slightly, before changing lanes. An LGV occupies much of the available lane width already and any move away from a mid-lane position may cause an overtaking driver or rider to assume that you're starting to pull out into their path.

Blind spots

You might not be able to see much by looking round, especially if the vehicle is fitted with a sleeper cab. This is all the more reason for being continually aware of vehicles just to the rear on either the offside or the nearside in blind-spot positions.

A quick sideways glance is often helpful, especially

- before changing lanes on a motorway or dual carriageway
- where traffic is merging from the right or the left
- when approaching the main carriageway from a motorway slip road.

Observation at junctions

Despite having a higher seating position than most drivers there will still be some junctions where your view is restricted by parked vehicles.

If it's possible, look through the windows of these vehicles, or if there are shops opposite, look for reflections in the windows. If you're still unable to see any oncoming traffic you'll have to ease forward until you can see properly. Do this without encroaching too far into the path of approaching traffic.

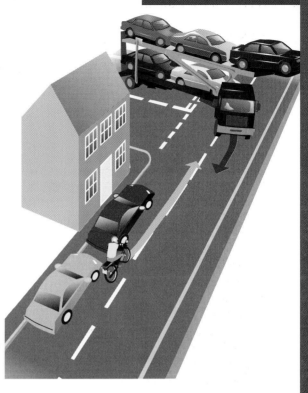

Some road users are more difficult to see than others, particularly cyclists, who will generally be approaching close to the kerb from the right. Motorcyclists are often difficult to see and can be travelling fast. Assess the situation. Don't emerge until you *know* that it's clear.

Pedestrians can often act unpredictably at junctions, just stepping or even running out, oblivious to your presence. Take in the whole scene before you commit yourself to moving a large (and frequently long) vehicle out across the path of oncoming traffic.

If you don't know, don't go

Zones of vision

As an LGV licence-holder your eyesight must be of a high standard. A skilful driver should be constantly scanning the road ahead and interpreting what's happening or likely to happen.

Always be aware of what's behind and alongside you. Use your peripheral vision to see changes 'out of the corner of your eye' before reacting to them. Look out for the possibility of

- vehicles about to emerge
- children running out
- other pedestrians stepping out.

Safe distances

Never drive at such a speed that you can't
pull up safely in the distance that you can
see to be clear. This should be irrespective of

- weather
- the road surface
- any load.

Don't drive beyond the limits of your vision.

Keep a safe separation distance between
you and the vehicle in front. In reasonable
weather conditions leave at least 1 metre
(about 3 feet) per mph of your speed, or a
two-second time gap. In poor weather, on
wet roads, you'll need to at least double the
distance, so allow a four-second time gap.

Look well ahead

Look well ahead for stop lights. On a road
with the national speed limit in force or on
the motorway, watch for other vehicles'
hazard warning lights. These might be
flashing to indicate that traffic ahead is
slowing down sharply for some reason.

The two-second rule

You can check the time gap by watching the vehicle in front pass an object such as a bridge, pole, sign, etc. and then saying to yourself

'Only a fool breaks the two-second rule'

You should have finished saying this by the time you reach the same spot. If you haven't finished the rhyme when you pass the spot, you're too close.

On some motorways this rule is drawn to drivers' attention by 'chevrons' painted on the road surface. The instruction 'Keep at least two chevrons from the vehicle ahead' also appears on a sign at these locations.

In congested traffic moving at slower speeds it may not be practicable to leave as much space, but you'll still need to leave enough distance in which to pull up safely.

If you find another vehicle driving too close behind you, gradually reduce your speed to increase any gap between you and a vehicle ahead. You'll then be able to brake more gently and remove the likelihood of the close-following vehicle running into the rear of your vehicle.

If another vehicle pulls into the safe separation gap that you're leaving, ease off your speed to extend the gap again.

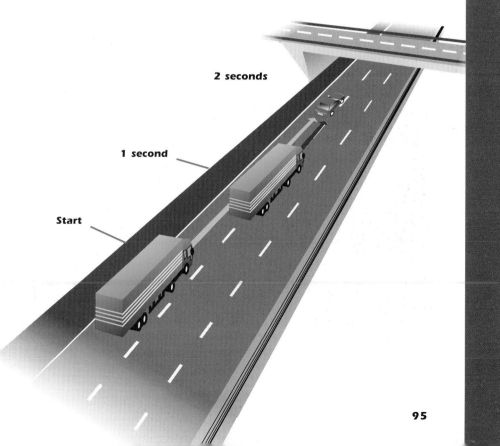

Traffic signals

By planning well ahead you'll ease some of the effort needed to drive an LGV.

Anticipating traffic speeds ahead and easing off the throttle means that you may be able to keep your vehicle moving. This will avoid the need to brake, to make a number of gear changes, to come to a stop, or to apply the handbrake. By driving like this you'll be able to make good progress and will keep down fuel costs.

Approaching traffic lights

Signals on green   Look well ahead and gauge how much traffic is waiting at each side of the junction you're approaching.

Ask yourself

- How long has green been showing?
- If the signals change, am I driving at such a speed that I can stop safely?
- If I have to brake hard, will following traffic be able to stop safely?
- Are there any vehicles waiting to turn across my path?
- How are the road surface and weather conditions going to affect the vehicle's braking distance?

Signals on amber   The amber signal means STOP. You may only continue if you

- have already crossed the stop line

- are so close to the stop line that to pull up might be unsafe or cause an accident.

Signals on red   The red traffic signal means that you must stop. You may be able to time your approach so that you're able to keep the vehicle moving as the signals change. This is especially important when driving a laden vehicle uphill to traffic signals. Look well ahead.

Signals not working   If you come upon traffic signals that aren't working, or there's a sign to show that they're out of order, treat the location as you would an unmarked junction and proceed with great care.

Remember, a green light means 'go on if the way is clear.' Check the junction to make sure other traffic using the junction is stopping at their red light. Only proceed on a green light if you can clear the junction.

Don't

- accelerate to try to 'beat' the signals
- leave it until the last moment to apply the brakes – harsh braking could result in loss of control.

Harsh accelerating or braking could also cause your load to move.

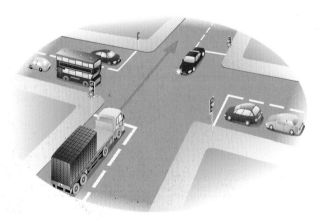

Signalling

You should signal to

- warn others of your intentions, especially if this involves a manoeuvre not readily apparent to other road users
- help other road users.

Road users include

- drivers of oncoming vehicles
- drivers of following vehicles
- motorcyclists
- cyclists
- crossing supervisors
- police directing traffic
- pedestrians
- horse riders
- road-repair contractors.

Give signals

- clearly and in good time
- that are illustrated in *The Highway Code*.

Your signals should be readily understood by all other road users. Try not to mislead others by giving signals that could confuse, especially when intending to pull up just after a road on the left. Another road user might misunderstand the meaning of the signal. In situations like this you should use your common sense and be ready for others' actions.

Don't use the headlights as a signal to give or claim priority. This might lead other vehicles into a hazardous situation.

Any signal that doesn't appear in *The Highway Code* is unauthorised and could be open to misinterpretation by another road user.

Using the horn

There are few instances when you'll need to sound the horn. Use it only if you

- assess that another road user may not be aware of your presence, thus avoiding possible danger
- need to warn other road users of your presence – at blind bends or a humpback bridge, for example

Sounding the horn doesn't

- give you priority
- relieve you of the responsibility to drive safely.

Don't use the horn

- when stationary
- at night between 11.30 pm and 7 am in a built-up area, unless there's danger from a moving vehicle
- as a rebuke or simply to attract attention (unless to avoid an accident).

Avoid long, aggressive blasts on the horn, which can alarm pedestrians. In any case, some pedestrians might be deaf.

Driving through tunnels

On approaching and in a tunnel

- switch on your dipped headlights
- do not wear sunglasses
- observe the road signs and signals
- keep an appropriate distance from the vehicle in front
- switch on your radio and tune to the indicated frequency.

If the tunnel is congested

- switch on your hazard warning lights
- keep your distance, even if you are moving slowly or stationary
- if possible, listen to messages on the radio
- follow any instructions given by tunnel officials or variable message signs.

If you break down or have an accident in a tunnel

- switch on your hazard warning lights
- switch off the engine
- leave your vehicle
- give first aid to any injured people, if you are able
- call for help from an emergency point.

If your vehicle is on fire and you can drive it out of the tunnel, do so. If not

- pull over to the side and switch off the engine
- leave the vehicle immediately
- DO NOT open the bonnet fully
- using the vehicle's extinguisher you may be able to direct the nozzle through the small gap available when the release catch on the bonnet is undone,
- If the fire appears to be large DO NOT try to tackle it, get well clear of the vehicle and leave it to the fire brigade
- DO NOT take any risks.

Driving at night

Problems encountered

Driving an LGV at night, often over long distances, requires additional skills. It also places added responsibilities on the driver.

The problems related to driving at night are

- much less advance information
- limited lighting (street lights or vehicle lights only)
- the headlights of oncoming vehicles
- shadows created by patchy street lighting
- ineffective lighting on other vehicles, pedal cycles, etc.
- dangers created by the onset of tiredness.

Many deaths have occurred because the driver of a large vehicle either was overcome by tiredness or failed to see an unlit broken-down vehicle until it was too late. Long night journeys, particularly on motorway routes with little to relieve the monotony, require planning and close attention to proper rest and refreshment stops.

Tiredness

Falling asleep at the wheel can happen for only a second or two and yet result in the loss of control.

Be on your guard.

Don't

- drive without a proper rest period
- allow the cab to become too warm
- eat heavy meals just before setting out
- take your eyes off the road to change radio channels or to change a tape, or a compact disc
- use a mobile phone when driving or use headphones.

Try to

- keep plenty of cool fresh air moving through the cab
- walk around in the fresh air during a rest stop before setting off again.

If you feel your concentration slipping, pull up at the next safe, convenient place.

Night vision

An LGV driver is required to have a better standard of eyesight than other road users. Make sure that your night vision matches up to this higher standard. Have your eyesight checked regularly and avoid

- wearing tinted glasses at night
- using windscreen or window tinting sprays.

Lighting-up time

You should be prepared to switch on whichever vehicle lights are appropriate to the conditions, regardless of the official lighting-up times. If the weather conditions are poor or it becomes overcast early, switch on your lights. See and be seen.

You must drive at an appropriate speed so that you can stop in the distance which you can see to be clear. In most cases that will be within the distance illuminated by your headlights or by street lights.

Unlit vehicles

Vehicles under 1,525 kg are permitted to park in 30 mph zones without lights at night time. Be on the alert when driving in built-up areas, especially when the street lighting is patchy.

Builders' skips are required to be lit and show reflective plates to oncoming traffic. Both of these measures can be either neglected or subject to vandalism, so watch out for unlit skips.

Adjusting to darkness

When you step out from a brightly lit area into darkness, such as when leaving a motorway service area, your eyes will take a short while to adjust to the different conditions. Use this time to check and clean your vehicle's lights, reflectors, lenses and mirrors.

At dawn

Other drivers may have been driving through the night and may also be less alert. Leave your lights on until you're satisfied that other road users will see you coming.

It's harder to judge speed and distance correctly in the half-light at dusk and dawn. The colour of some vehicles makes them harder to see in half-light conditions. Switch on your lights to ensure that others can see you.

See and be seen.

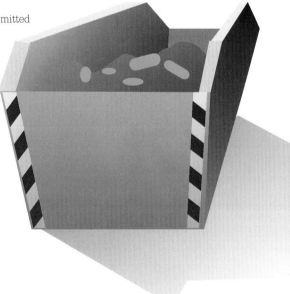

Vehicle lighting

It's essential that all lamps are clean and bulbs and light units are operating correctly. In addition to the driver being able to see ahead properly, it's essential that other road users are able to recognise the size of your vehicle and its direction of travel.

All regulation markers and rear lights must be lit and clear of dirt and obstructions such as ropes, sheets, overhanging projections, etc. If you have permission to move any load at night that projects beyond the normal size of the vehicle, all additional marker lights and hazards lights should be on.

Oversized loads are usually in lay-bys, etc. overnight. However, in certain circumstances the police authority responsible for that particular area may consider the load would be more safely moved when there's less traffic on the road. Look for any signals given by the escort of such vehicles.

Avoid the 'Christmas tree' effect seen on some vehicles. It can be distracting and confusing to other road users at night. Also, any red light used in the cab must not show to the front of the vehicle.

Auxiliary lighting

LGV drivers must conform to regulations governing the use and fitting of any auxiliary lamps, especially with regard to their mounting height from the road surface. It's an offence to use fog lights or spotlights whose centres are less than 0.6 metres (2 feet) from the ground, except in poor weather conditions such as mist, fog or falling snow.

Any lights showing to the front should be white (or, as allowed on some vehicles, yellow) unless they're side marker lights, required to be fitted by law to certain longer vehicles.

If your vehicle is fitted with any additional working lights to assist coupling/uncoupling, loading, etc., remember to switch them off when the vehicle is out on the road.

High-intensity rear fog lights and additional front fog lights should only be used when visibility is less than 100 metres (about 330 feet). They must be switched off when the visibility improves.

Amber hazard lights are required, depending on the load projecting beyond specified limits or the vehicle travelling at slower speeds than normal.

Parked vehicles

All LGVs must have lights on when parked on the road at night. A lay-by is usually within the specified distance from any carriageway, so lights are still required.

Unless your vehicle is in an 'off-street' parking location, such as a lorry park, it must be clearly lit to comply with the law.

Driving in built-up areas

Always use dipped headlights in built-up areas at night. It helps others to see you and assists your vision if the street lighting varies or is defective.

Be on the alert for

- pedestrians in dark clothing
- runners
- cyclists (often with poor lighting).

Take extra care when approaching pedestrian crossings. Drive at such a speed that you can stop safely if necessary.

Make sure that you still obey the speed limits even if the roads appear to be empty.

Maintenance work

Essential maintenance work is often carried out at night time. Be on the alert for diversion signs, obstructions and coned-off sections of road when you're driving at night time.

Street cleansing often takes place at night in larger cities, so be on the lookout for slow-moving vehicles.

Driving in rural areas

If there's no oncoming traffic you should use full beam headlights to see as far ahead as possible. Dip your lights as soon as you see oncoming traffic to avoid dazzling the oncoming driver or rider.

If there's no footpath, be on the alert for pedestrians in the road. *The Highway Code* advises pedestrians to walk facing oncoming traffic in these situations, but not all pedestrians follow this advice.

Additionally, *The Highway Code* advises large groups of people on organised walks that they should walk on the left.

Fog at night

If there's any possibility of fog developing at night *don't drive*.

If the fog becomes so dense that you're unable to go any further safely, your vehicle will present a serious hazard to other vehicles. Because of the difficulties of getting an LGV off the road in dense fog, it's better not to start out in the first place.

If you start your journey when there's fog about and you're delayed, you'll be committing an offence if you exceed the permitted hours of driving for that period, because the delay was foreseeable.

Overtaking at night

Because LGVs take some considerable time to complete an overtaking manoeuvre you must only attempt one when you can see well ahead that it's safe to do so.

This means that unless you're driving on a motorway or dual carriageway the opportunities to overtake will be limited. Without street lighting you won't be able to assess if there are bends, junctions, hills, etc., which may prevent you seeing an oncoming vehicle.

If you do decide to overtake, make sure that you can do so without 'cutting in'

on the vehicle being overtaken, or causing oncoming vehicles to brake or swerve.

Never close up on the vehicle ahead prior to attempting to overtake. This will restrict your vision of the road ahead.

Separation distance

Avoid driving so close to the vehicle ahead that your lights dazzle the other driver. Make sure that your lights are on dipped beam.

If a vehicle overtakes you, dip your headlights as soon as the vehicle starts to pass you. Your headlights should fall short of the vehicle in front.

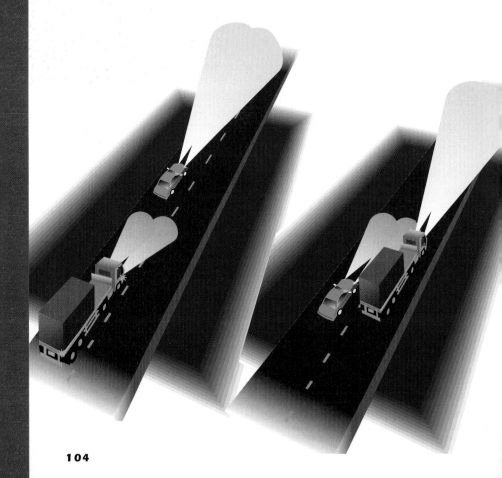

Breakdowns

If your vehicle breaks down, try to pull it as far off to the left as possible. If you can get off the main carriageway without causing danger or inconvenience to other road users, especially pedestrians, do so. But don't park on the pavement: the weight of an LGV can damage paving stones and underground services.

If you have a warning triangle, place it at least 45 metres (147 feet) behind the vehicle on normal roads. Some form of warning is vital if an electrical problem has put the rear lights out of action. However, don't attempt to place a warning triangle or any other warning device on a motorway carriageway, hard shoulder or slip road.

Don't attempt to work on the offside of the vehicle unless protected by a recovery vehicle with flashing hazard lights. Even then, take great care on roads carrying fast-moving traffic. Injuries and fatalities have occurred at the scenes of initially simple breakdowns.

If your vehicle is causing an obstruction and possible danger to other road users inform the police as soon as possible. This is particularly important if your vehicle is carrying dangerous goods or other hazardous materials.

If you suspect that your vehicle has a mechanical problem, don't be tempted to continue on your journey. Small defects could become dangerous if they're left without attention. You could also end up creating traffic chaos if your vehicle eventually breaks down in a difficult location.

Recovery agencies

If you're engaged in long-distance work, especially at night, it's wise to ensure that the vehicle is covered by a reputable recovery agency. The cost of towing or repairing an LGV could be substantial without the benefit of recovery membership.

For safety reasons, vehicles that break down on the motorway are required to be removed as quickly as possible.

Motorway driving

Basic preparation

Motorways are statistically the safest road systems in the UK. However, motorway accidents invariably involve a larger number of vehicles travelling at high speeds and usually result in more serious injuries and damage than incidents on normal roads.

Because of the high numbers of such vehicles using the motorway network's inter-city links, many of these accidents involve LGVs. But if everyone who used the motorway drove to the same high standard that's required of LGV drivers, it's arguable that many of these incidents could be avoided.

The higher overall speeds and the volume of traffic cause conditions to change much more rapidly than on normal roads. For this reason you need to be

- totally alert
- physically fit
- concentrating fully.

If you aren't, you may not be able to react to any sudden change taking place ahead of you.

Fitness

Don't drive if you're

- tired
- unwell
- taking flu remedies, etc.
- worried
- unable to concentrate.

Any of these factors will affect your reactions, especially if you have to deal with an emergency.

Rest periods

You must observe mandatory rest periods in your daily driving schedule. On long journeys, try to plan them to coincide with a break at a motorway service area or refreshment stop. This is especially important at night, when a long journey can cause tiredness to set in.

It's illegal to stop anywhere on the motorway hard shoulder or slip roads for a rest. If you feel tiredness coming on, open the windows, turn the heating down and get off the motorway at the next junction. When you get to a service area, have a hot drink, wash your face (to refresh you) and walk round in the fresh air before driving on.

Bear in mind that a substantial meal accompanied by the warmth in the cab, the continual resonance of the engine and long, uninterrupted stretches of road, especially at night, can produce the very conditions you need to avoid.

Regulations

Motorways are subject to specific rules and regulations that must be observed by all LGV drivers. Study those sections relating to motorways in *The Highway Code*. You also need to know, understand and obey motorway warning signs and signals.

Vehicle checks

Before driving on the motorway you should ensure that you carry out routine checks on your vehicle, especially considering the long distances and prolonged higher speeds involved. For fuller details on vehicle maintenance, see page 41.

Tyres

All tyres on your vehicle (and any trailer) must be in good condition. Tyres can become very hot and may disintegrate under sustained high-speed running. Check for excessive heat when you stop for a break.

Inspect both the inside and outside visible faces for signs of

- wear
- damage
- bulges
- separation
- exposed cords.

Make sure that your vehicle has the correct-sized wheels fitted. Smaller diameters will run faster and may overheat on longer journeys. Ensure that all tyres are suitable for the loads being carried.

If a tyre bursts or shreds you may be able to see this in your mirrors. If you see smoke from the tyres you should stop as soon as it's safe to do so.

Also, make a habit of checking the tyre pressures regularly.

Mirrors

Ensure that all mirrors are properly adjusted to give the best possible view to the rear. They should also be clean. The simple device of tying a piece of cloth to the mirror bracket cleans them effectively as the air flow causes it to continually wipe the surface. Make sure that you tie it on tightly so that it doesn't work free and fly off.

Windscreen

All glass must be

- clean
- clear
- free from defects.

Keep all windscreen washer reservoirs topped up and the jets clear. Make sure that all wiper blades are in good condition.

Spray-suppression equipment

It's essential that you check all spray-suppression equipment fitted to the vehicle and any trailer before setting out, especially if bad weather is expected.

Instruments

Check all gauges and warning lights such as

- anti-lock brakes (ABS)
- air pressure
- oil pressure
- coolant
- temperature
- lights.

Lights and indicators

To comply with the law all lights must be in working order even in daylight. Make sure that all bulbs, headlight units, lenses and reflectors are fitted, clean and function as intended.

High-intensity rear fog lights and marker lights (if fitted) must operate correctly. Indicator lights must operate and 'flash' within the specified frequency range. Reversing lights must either automatically operate by the selection of reverse gear or be switched on from the cab with a warning light to show when they're lit.

Fuel

Make sure that you either have enough fuel on board to complete the journey or have the facility (cash, agency card, etc.) to refuel at a service area.

Oil

The engine operates at sustained high speeds on a motorway, so it's vital to check all oil levels before setting out. Running low can result in costly damage to the engine and could cause a breakdown at a dangerous location.

Coolant

The engine will be running for sustained periods so it's essential to check the levels of coolant in the system.

Joining a motorway

There are three alternative ways in which traffic can join a motorway. All these access routes will be clearly signed.

At a roundabout

The exit from a roundabout will be signposted. Signs are displayed prominently to prevent non-motorway traffic accidentally entering the system.

Main trunk road becomes a motorway

There will be prominent advance warning signs so that prohibited traffic can leave the main route before the motorway regulations apply.

Via a slip road

Slip roads leading directly onto the motorway will be clearly signed to prevent prohibited traffic entering the motorway.

Effective observation   Before joining the motorway from a slip road try to assess what traffic conditions are like on the motorway itself. You may be able to do this as you approach from a distance or if you need to reach the entry point by means of an over-bridge.

Get as much advance information as you can to help plan your speed on the slip road. You'll need to build up your speed and emerge safely onto the main carriageway.

Plan your approach and try to avoid having to stop at the end of the slip road. But if the motorway is extremely busy you may *have to* stop and filter into the traffic. Don't use the size of your vehicle to force your way onto the motorway. Use your mirror and signal as you pull out onto the main carriageway, if it's safe to do so.

A quick sideways glance may be necessary to ensure that you correctly assess the speed of any traffic approaching in the nearside lane. Don't

- pull out into the path of traffic in the nearside lane if this will cause it to slow down or swerve
- drive along the hard shoulder to 'filter' into the left-hand lane.

There are a small number of locations where traffic merges onto the motorway from the right. Take extra care in these situations.

Making progress approaching access points

After passing a motorway exit there will often be an entrance or access point onto the motorway. Look well ahead and if there are vehicles joining the motorway

- don't try to race them while they're on the slip road
- be prepared to adjust your speed
- move to the next lane, if it's safe to do so, to allow joining traffic to merge.

Lane discipline

Keep to the left-hand lane unless overtaking slower vehicles. LGVs aren't allowed in the extreme right-hand lane on a three-lane or multi-lane motorway, unless there are road-works or signs that indicate otherwise. On two-lane motorways LGVs are permitted to use the right-hand lane for overtaking.

Use the MSM/PSL routine well before signalling to move out. Don't start to pull out and then signal.

On a three- or four-lane motorway make sure that you check for any vehicle in the right-hand lane(s) that might be about to move back to the left. Most of the traffic coming up behind will be travelling at a much higher speed.

Look well ahead to plan any overtaking manoeuvre, especially given the effect a speed limiter will have on the power available to you.

Observe signs showing a crawler/climber lane for LGVs. This will suggest a long, gradual climb ahead.

If a slow-moving oversized load is being escorted, look for any signal the escort might give. They may permit you to move into the right-hand lane to pass the obstruction.

If a motorway lane merges from the right (in a few cases only) you should move over to the left as soon as it's safe to do so. At these specific locations no offence is committed if an LGV is initially travelling in the extreme right-hand lane. Move over to the left as soon as it's safe to do so.

Separation distance

On motorways you should allow

- greater margins than on normal roads
- a safe separation distance.

In good conditions you'll need at least

- a stopping distance of one metre (about 3 feet 3 inches) for every mph
- a two-second separation gap from the vehicle in front.

In poor conditions you'll need at least

- double the stopping distance
- a four-second separation gap from the vehicle in front.

In snow or icy conditions the stopping distances can be **ten times** those needed in normal dry conditions.

Seeing and being seen

Make sure that you start out with a clean windscreen, mirrors and windows. Use the washers, wipers and demisters to keep the screen clear. In poor conditions use dipped headlights.

Keep reassessing traffic conditions around you. Watch out for brake lights or hazard warning lights that show the traffic ahead is either stationary or slowing down.

High-intensity rear fog lights should only be used when visibility falls below 100 metres (about 330 feet). They should be switched off when visibility improves, unless fog is patchy and danger still exists.

Motorway signs and signals

Motorway signs are larger than normal road signs. They can be read from greater distances and can help you to plan ahead.

Know your intended route. Be ready for the exit that you need to use and prepare for it in good time, well before you reach it.

Where there are major roadworks there may be diversions for LGVs in operation. Look for the yellow

* square
* diamond
* circle
* triangle

symbols combined with capital route letters. Follow the symbol on the route signs.

Signals

Warning lights show when there are dangers ahead such as

* accidents
* fog
* icy roads.

Look out for variable message warning signs advising

* lane closures
* speed limits
* hazards
* standing traffic ahead.

You need to comply with advisory speed limit signs shown on the motorway hazard warning lights matrix.

Red light signals If the red X signals show above your lane don't go beyond the red light

* be ready to comply with any signs that tell you to change lanes
* be ready to leave the motorway
* observe brake lights or flashing hazard warning lights, which show that there's stationary or very slow-moving traffic ahead.

React in good time

Lane control
signals ahead
↓ lane open
✕ lane closed
↙ move to left

Weather conditions

Because of the higher speeds on motorways it's important to take into account any effects the weather may have on driving conditions. Listen to weather forecasts on the radio.

Rain

Visibility can be reduced by the spray thrown up by numbers of LGVs travelling at speed. You should

- use headlights so that other drivers can see you
- reduce speed when the road surface is wet. You need to be able to pull up in the distance that you can see to be clear
- leave a greater separation gap. Use the four-second rule as a minimum
- make sure that all spray-suppression equipment fitted to your vehicle is effective
- take extra care when the road surface is wet after rain. The roads may still be slippery even if the sun is out.

Crosswinds

Be aware of the effects strong crosswinds can have on other road users. Watch out especially

- after passing motorway bridges
- on elevated exposed sections
- when passing vehicles towing caravans, horse boxes, etc.

If you're driving a high-sided vehicle such as a

- furniture removal van (pantechnicon)
- box van carrying comparatively light merchandise
- curtain-sided vehicle

take special notice of warnings for drivers of such vehicles. Avoid known problem areas such as viaducts, high suspension bridges, etc.

Motorcyclists are especially vulnerable to severe crosswinds on motorways, so allow room when overtaking them. Check the nearside mirror to observe them after you've overtaken.

Ice or frost

In cold weather, especially at night when temperatures can drop suddenly, be on the alert for any feeling of lightness in the steering. This may suggest frost or ice on the road. Watch for signs of frost along the hard shoulder as well. A warm cab can isolate you from the real conditions outside.

Motorways that appear wet may in fact be frozen. There are devices that fix onto the exterior mirror to show when the outside temperature drops below freezing.

Allow up to **ten times** the normal distance for braking in icy conditions. Remember, all braking should be carried out gently to reduce the risk of losing control.

Fog

If there's fog on the motorway you must reduce speed so that you can pull up in the distance that you can see to be clear. You should

- slow down
- use dipped headlights
- use rear high-intensity fog lights if visibility is less than 100 metres (about 330 feet)
- stay back
- check your speedometer.

Don't

- speed up again if the fog is patchy. You could run into dense fog again within a short distance
- hang onto the rear lights of the vehicle in front.

Fog affects your judgement of speed and distance. You may be travelling faster than you realise.

Slow down

Multiple pile-ups on motorways don't just happen – they're caused by drivers who

- travel too fast
- drive too close
- assume there's nothing stopped ahead
- ignore signals.

You can't see well ahead in fog

If you see fog warning signs but visibility is clear, there may be foggy conditions ahead. Be prepared and reduce speed in good time.

When driving in fog, watch out for any signals that tell you to leave the motorway. Also, look for accidents ahead and for emergency vehicles coming up behind (possibly on the hard shoulder). Police cars may be parked on the hard shoulder with their lights flashing. This might mean that traffic has stopped on the carriageway ahead.

'Motorway madness' is the term used to describe the behaviour of those reckless drivers who drive too fast for the conditions. The police prosecute drivers after serious multiple accidents. This is to get the message across to all drivers that they must

slow down in fog

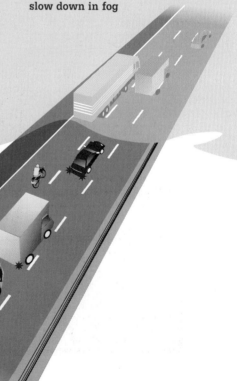

Contraflows and roadworks

Essential roadworks involving opposite streams of traffic sharing one carriageway are known as contraflow systems. The object is to permit traffic to continue moving while repairs or resurfacing take place on the other carriageway or lanes.

Red and white marker posts are used to separate opposite streams of traffic. The normal white lane-marking reflective studs are replaced by temporary yellow/green fluorescent studs.

A 50 mph mandatory speed limit is usually imposed over the stretch affected. This means a closing speed of 100 mph in the event of a collision. When you are driving in roadworks or contraflow areas, you should

- concentrate on what's going on ahead
- keep a safe separation distance from the vehicle in front
- look well ahead to avoid the need to brake sharply
- comply with advance warning signs, which indicate lanes that must not be used by LGVs (this applies to vehicles over 7.5 tonnes MAM)
- avoid sudden steering movements or any sharp braking.

You should not

- let the activity on the closed section distract you
- exceed the speed limit
- change lanes if signs tell you to stay in your lane
- speed up until you reach the end of the roadworks and normal motorway speed limits apply again.

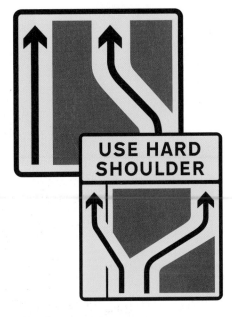

Accidents

Serious accidents can often occur when vehicles cross into the path of the other traffic stream in a contraflow. You must

- keep your speed down
- keep your distance
- stay alert.

Signs

Take notice of advance warning signs (often starting five miles before the roadworks). Get into the correct lane in good time and don't force your way in at the last moment.

Drivers of LGVs carrying oversized loads MUST comply with the advance warning notices. These will tell you either to leave the motorway or to stop and telephone the police and wait for an escort through the roadworks.

Breakdowns

If your vehicle breaks down in a roadworks section, remain with the vehicle. These sections of motorway are usually under TV monitoring. A recovery vehicle, which is provided free of charge in the roadworks section, will be with you as soon as possible.

Be on the lookout for broken-down vehicles causing an obstruction ahead.

Breakdowns on the motorway

If your vehicle develops a problem, leave the motorway at the next exit or pull into a service area. If you can't do this, pull onto the hard shoulder and stop as far to the left as possible

- don't attempt even minor repairs on the motorway
- switch on the hazard warning lights
- make sure that the vehicle lights are on at night time, unless an electrical fault prevents this.

You must not place a warning triangle or any other warning device on the motorway carriageway, hard shoulder or slip road.

Emergency telephones

Motorway emergency telephones are free and easily located. You'll be connected directly to the motorway police control centre, who will then get in touch with a recovery company for you.

In most cases the emergency telephones are 1.6 km (about 1 mile) apart. The direction of the nearest phone will be shown by the arrow on the marker posts along the edge of the hard shoulder. Don't cross the carriageway or any slip road to get to a telephone. Face the oncoming traffic while using the telephone.

If your vehicle has its own telephone, or you use a mobile phone to contact the police, identify your location from the marker posts on the hard shoulder before you phone.

If anything falls from either your vehicle or another vehicle

- use the nearest emergency telephone to call the police
- don't attempt to recover it yourself
- don't stand on the carriageway to warn oncoming traffic.

Leaving the motorway

Progressive signs will show upcoming exits. At one mile you'll see

- the junction number
- the road number
- the one-mile indicator.

Half a mile from the exit you'll see signs for

- the main town or city served by the exit
- the junction number
- the road number
- the half-mile exit.

Finally, 300 yards (270 metres) before the exit there will be three countdown markers every 100 yards.

A driver of a vehicle travelling at 60 mph has only 60 seconds from the one-mile sign to the exit. So even at a speed of 50 mph there's still only 80 seconds from the one-mile sign to the actual exit.

Plan well in advance in order to be in the left-hand lane in good time. Large vehicles in the left-hand lane may prevent a driver in the second lane from seeing the one-mile sign, leaving very little time to move to the left safely.

You must use the MSM/PSL routine in good time before changing lanes or signalling. Assess the speed of traffic ahead in good time in order to avoid overtaking and then having to pull back in and reduce speed to leave at the next exit. Don't

- pull across at the last moment
- drive over the white chevrons that divide the slip road from the main carriageway.

Occasionally there are several exits close together, or a service area close to an exit. Look well ahead and plan your exit in good time. Watch out for other drivers' mistakes, especially those leaving it too late to exit safely.

Traffic queuing

At some locations traffic can be held up on the slip road. Look well ahead and be prepared for this. Don't queue on the hard shoulder.

Illuminated signs have been introduced at a number of such locations to give advance warning messages of traffic queuing on the slip road or in the first lane. Watch out for indicators and hazard warning flashers when traffic is held up ahead.

Use the MSM/PSL routine in good time and move to the second lane if you aren't leaving by such an exit.

End of the motorway

There are 'End of Motorway' regulation signs

- at the end of slip roads
- where the road becomes a normal main road.

These remind you that different rules apply to the road that you're joining. Watch out for signs advising you of

- speed limits
- dual carriageways
- two-way traffic
- clearways
- motorway link roads
- part-time traffic signals.

Reduce speed

After driving on the motorway for some time it's easy to become accustomed to the speed. When you first leave the motorway, 40 or 45 mph can seem more like 20 mph. You should

- adjust your driving to the new conditions as soon as possible
- check the speedometer to see the real speed.

Start reducing speed when you're clear of the main carriageway. Motorway slip or link roads often have sharp curves that need to be taken at lower speeds.

Look well ahead for traffic queuing at a roundabout or traffic signals. Be prepared for the change in traffic at the end of the motorway. Look out for

- pedestrians
- cyclists, etc.

All-weather driving

Goods need to be delivered 24 hours a day all year round. With that in mind, you should employ safe driving techniques to ensure that you, your vehicle and the goods in your care always arrive safely at their destination with the minimum of delay. You'll need all your skills to achieve this objective during periods of bad weather.

It's essential that you take notice of warnings of severe weather such as

- snow or blizzard conditions
- floods
- fog
- high winds.

If an LGV becomes stranded the road may well be blocked for essential rescue and medical services. In the case of fog it could result in other vehicles behind colliding with the stranded vehicle.

Training and preparation are vital. Don't venture out in severe weather conditions without being properly prepared.

Your vehicle

Your vehicle must be in a fit and proper condition at all times. This means regular safety checks and strict observance of maintenance schedules. For fuller details on vehicle maintenance, see page 41.

Tyres

Check the tread depth and pattern. LGVs must have a tread depth of at least 1mm across three-quarters of the breadth of the tread and in a continuous band around the entire circumference. Examine tyres for cuts, damage and signs of cord visible at the side walls.

Brakes

It's essential that the brakes are operating correctly at all times. Any imbalance could cause a skid if the brakes are applied on a slippery surface.

Oil and fuel

Use the correct grades of fuel and oil for any extreme conditions.

Prolonged hot weather will place additional demands on the lubricating oil in engines and turbo-chargers. In extremes of cold it will be necessary to use diesel fuel with 'anti-waxing' additives to prevent fuel lines freezing up.

In excessively dusty conditions, which can be encountered on construction sites, quarries, etc., you should strictly follow schedules relating to filter changes.

Icy weather

Ensure the whole of the windscreen is cleared before attempting to move off in frosty conditions.

If you're driving at night time be alert for any drop in temperature that could cause untreated roads to become icy. If the steering feels light you're probably driving on a frozen road surface, so ease your speed as soon as it's safe to do so. All braking must be gentle and over much longer distances, especially when driving articulated vehicles or those with a trailer.

You'll have to allow more time for the journey because overall speeds will need to be lower. Also, keep a safe separation distance from any vehicle ahead. Allow **ten times** the normal stopping distance.

Drive sensibly and allow for the fact that other road users might get into difficulties. Avoid any sudden braking, steering or acceleration.

Heavy rain

Ensure that the wipers are clearing the windscreen properly – you'll need to be able to see clearly ahead. Make sure that the screen is also demisted efficiently and that the washer containers are filled with suitable fluid, especially in winter conditions.

Allow at least twice as much separation distance as you would in dry conditions. If you must brake, do it while the vehicle is stable and preferably travelling in a straight line. Avoid sudden or harsh braking.

Obey advisory speed limit signs on motorways.

Other road users will have more difficulty seeing when there's heavy rain and spray. Make sure that all spray-suppression equipment on your vehicle is secure and operating.

Don't use high-intensity rear fog lights unless visibility is less than 100 metres (330 feet).

Construction sites

Heavy rain can turn construction sites into quagmires. Take care when driving on off-road gradients, or when getting down from the cab.

If the vehicle is fitted with a switch for locking up the differential mechanism on the drive axle (the 'diff-lock'), engage it. This will ensure that the power is transmitted to all driven wheels and will assist traction by eliminating wheelspin. Remember to disengage the diff-lock as soon as you return to normal road surfaces again.

It's an offence to deposit mud on the roadway to the extent that it could endanger other road users. This may involve hosing down the wheels and undergear of your vehicle before it leaves such a site. You should also check between double wheels before leaving the site for any large stones or building bricks wedged between the tyres. Such objects can fly out at speed, with serious consequences for following traffic.

Snow

Falling snow can reduce visibility dramatically. Use dipped headlights and reduce your speed. Allow a much greater stopping and separation distance – up to *ten times* the stopping distance on dry roads.

Road markings and traffic signs can become obscured by snow. Take extra care at junctions.

Deep snow as a result of drifting in high winds can often lead to the closure of high-level roads. Don't attempt to use such roads if

- broadcasts tell LGV drivers to avoid those routes
- warning signs indicate that the road is closed to LGVs or other traffic
- severe weather conditions are forecast.

Some rural roads in exposed places have marker posts at the side of the road that will give a guide to the depth of the snow.

In prolonged periods of snow the fixing of snow chains to driven wheels will often prove to be of value. Remember, a stranded LGV could

- prevent snow ploughs clearing the route
- delay emergency vehicles
- block the road for other road users.

Ploughs and gritting vehicles

Don't attempt to overtake a snow plough or gritting vehicle. You may find yourself running into deep snow or skidding on an untreated section of roadway which these maintenance vehicles could have cleared or treated had you followed on behind them. Keep well back from gritting vehicles. If they're on the road there could be bad weather on the way.

Deep snow

If your vehicle becomes stuck in deep snow, engage the diff-lock (if one is fitted) to regain forward traction. Switch it off as soon as the vehicle is moving and before attempting a turn.

Another technique for freeing a vehicle stuck in the snow is to use the highest gear you can to improve traction. Then try alternating between reverse and the forward gear until forward motion is possible. Avoid continual revving in a low gear. This will only result in the drive wheels digging an even deeper rut.

It's often helpful to keep a couple of strong sacks in the cab to put under the drive wheels if the vehicle becomes stuck. A shovel is also handy if the journey is likely to involve crossing areas where snow is known to be a hazard during the winter.

When operating independent retarders care must be taken on the descent of snow-covered gradients. The retarders could cause the rear wheels to lock. Some retarders are managed by the ABS to help avoid this problem.

Fog

Don't drive in dense fog if you can postpone your journey and avoid driving at all at night-time if there is fog. Don't start a journey that might need to be abandoned because it becomes too dangerous to proceed any further.

The options for finding a safe place to park an LGV off the road in dense fog are limited. You must not leave an LGV on public roads where it would be a danger to other road users. Never leave any LGV or trailer without lights where it would endanger others.

Lights

Use dipped headlights in any reduced visibility. You need to see and be seen.

Use rear high-intensity fog lights and front fog lights when visibility is less than 100 metres (330 feet). Rear fog lights must only be capable of operating with dipped headlights or front fog lights. Switch off front and rear fog lights when visibility improves above 100 metres (330 feet), but beware of patchy fog.

Keep all lenses and reflectors clean. You may need to check more often in poor weather conditions. Ensure that all lights are working correctly.

In fog, don't

- drive too close to the centre of the road
- confuse centre lines and lane markings
- drive without using headlights
- speed up because the fog appears to thin out
- use full beam when following another vehicle – the shadows will make it difficult for the driver ahead to see.

A large vehicle travelling ahead of you may temporarily displace some of the fog, making it appear clearer than it really is. Then again, in a larger vehicle you may be able to see ahead over low-lying fog. Don't speed up in case there are smaller vehicles in front that may be hidden from view.

Slow down

- Don't speed up if the fog appears thinner. It could be patchy and you could run into it again.
- Keep checking the speedometer to see your true speed. Fog can make it difficult to judge speed and distance.

Stay back

- Keep a safe separation distance from any vehicle ahead.
- Don't speed up if a vehicle appears to be close behind.
- Only overtake if you can be *sure* the road ahead is clear.

Reflective studs and markings

Reflective studs are provided on dual carriageways to help drivers in poor visibility. The colours of reflective studs are

- **red** on the left-hand edge of carriageways
- **white** to indicate lane markings
- **green** at slip roads and lay-bys
- **amber** on the right-hand edge of carriageways and the centre reservation
- **fluorescent yellow/green** at roadwork contraflow systems.

On some rural roads there are black and white marker posts, with red reflectors on the left-hand side and white reflectors on the right-hand side of the road. The continuous white line between the left-hand lane and the hard shoulder, and at the left-hand edge of some trunk roads, incorporates a 'rumble' strip. This produces a vibration designed to warn drivers when their vehicle crosses the line.

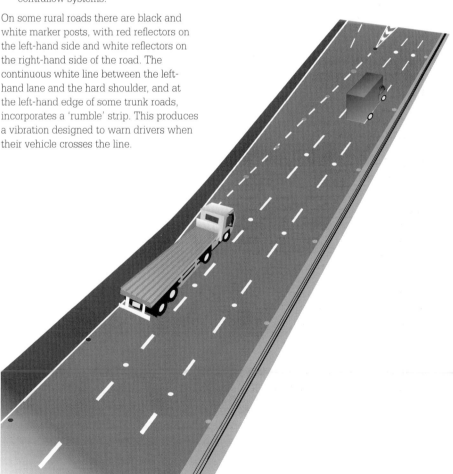

High winds

In severe weather conditions you should plan your journey well in advance (24 hours ahead, if possible). Listen to, watch or read the weather forecast, especially if you're the driver of

- a high-sided vehicle (removal vans, long wheel-base box vans, etc.)
- a vehicle with a curtain-side body or trailer
- a vehicle transporting portable buildings, etc. with large flat surfaces susceptible to wind pressures
- a vehicle towing a horse box
- an unladen van of any description.

Take notice if your route includes any locations that are frequently subjected to high winds such as

- high-level bridges or roads
- exposed viaducts
- exposed stretches of motorway.

Watch out for signs indicating high winds. Also, beware of fallen trees or damaged branches that could fall on your vehicle.

Take notice of advance warnings and always remember that

- the route may be closed to certain LGVs
- there may be additional delays due to lane closures. This is done on high-level bridges to create empty 'buffer' lanes, which cope with vehicles that are blown off course into the next lane
- you may need to use an alternative route
- if you ignore the warnings, your vehicle and its load could be affected by the strong winds and could place yourself and other road users in danger.

Bear in mind that ferry sailings are likely to be affected by gale force winds, resulting in delays or cancellation.

Other road users

In windy conditions other road users are likely to be affected when

- overtaking your vehicle
- you overtake them.

Check the nearside mirror(s) as you overtake to ensure that they still have control of their vehicle. In addition, be on the alert for vehicles or motorcyclists 'wandering' into your lane.

Don't ignore warnings of severe winds. If your vehicle is blown over you could delay the emergency services from reaching an even more serious incident.

Avoiding and dealing with congestion

The increasing level of vehicles on the roads has caused a level of congestion which can lead to frustration and increases in journey times. This affects urban areas, higher speed roads and motorways.

However, there is an opportunity for all drivers to help alleviate this problem to some extent, by changing their driving habits. Detailed below are ways to do this.

Journey Planning

Time of day

If possible, try to plan journeys to avoid the busy times of day. Much congestion is generated by work/school related travel, causing delays in the early morning and late afternoon/early evening. If you don't have to travel at these times try to avoid them. This will both ease the congestion caused by traffic governed by work/school schedules, and allow you an easier, more pleasant journey, less likely to experience delays.

Route planning

Make sure you know where you're going by planning beforehand. If possible, include alternatives into your plan in case you find your original route blocked especially if the route is unknown to you. You could

- use a map - you may need to use different scale maps depending on how far and where you're travelling

- consult a motoring organisation or use one of the route planners available on the internet

- print out or write down the route, using place names and road numbers to avoid problems if a certain place is not adequately signed.

Be aware of the size of your vehicle in relation to the width of certain accesses or narrow town roads - it can be very difficult or impossible to manoeuvre a large vehicle if, for example, a one way street or sharp turn is found to be too narrow, or where weight or height restrictions apply.

Your journey

Leave plenty of time, especially if you're connecting with other forms of transport. Concern about reaching your destination in time can lead to frustration and the increased tendency to take risks which in turn could lead to an accident. Delivery schedules need to allow for this so the driver isn't forced into taking unnecessary risks to stay on time. Carry your map or directions with you so you can check positions or identify alternative routes if you're delayed or diverted, but **don't** attempt to look at a map or read directions whilst driving.

A Global Positioning System (GPS) will identify your route for you.

Mobile phones

A mobile phone can be useful in case of delays or breakdowns. However, remember that it is illegal to use a hand held mobile phone whilst driving, including while you are waiting in a queue of traffic. Find a safe place to stop before making a call. If you are driving alone on a motorway, you must leave the motorway before using the phone.

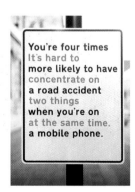

You're four times more likely to have a road accident when you're on a mobile phone.

Hazard perception

Looking well ahead to see what other road users in front of you are doing will enable you to plan your driving. If you see any changes that could cause you to slow down or alter course, ease off the accelerator and gradually slow down rather than leaving it late and having to brake harshly. Slow down early - the traffic situation ahead will often have cleared by the time you get there.

Constant Speed

When you can see well ahead and the road conditions are good, you should try to drive at a constant speed - this is the time to use cruise control if it is fitted to your vehicle.

Whether or not you have cruise control, choose a speed which is within the speed limit and one which you and your vehicle can handle safely. Make sure you also keep a safe distance from the vehicle in front. Remember to increase the gap on wet or icy roads. Also remember that, in foggy conditions, you will have to slow down to the distance you can see to be clear.

At busy times there are some stretches of motorway which have variable speed limits shown above the lanes. The maximum speed limits shown on these signals are mandatory and appear on the gantries above the lanes to which they apply.

These speed limits are in place to make traffic proceed at a constant speed as this has been shown to reduce bunching, and consequently, over a longer distance, congestion has been shown to ease. Your overall journey time normally improves by keeping to the constant speed, even though at times it may appear that you could have travelled faster for shorter periods.

Lane discipline

You should drive in the left-hand lane of a dual carriageway or motorway if the road ahead is clear.

If you are overtaking a number of slower-moving vehicles it may be safer to remain in the centre lane until the manoeuvre is completed rather than continually changing lanes. Return to the left-hand lane once you have overtaken all the vehicles or if you are delaying traffic behind you. Don't hog the middle lane especially if you are driving a vehicle over 7.5 tonnes. If you are overtaking another large vehicle, and the speed differential between the two is slight, this causes a slow overtake situation. This can delay other faster vehicles, and cause frustration which can lead to dangerous situations. It also means that you are effectively turning a three-lane motorway into a two-lane motorway.

You must not normally drive on the hard shoulder, but at road works and certain places where signs direct, the hard shoulder may become the left lane.

Using Sign information

Look well ahead for signals or signs, especially on a motorway. Signals situated on the central reservation apply to all lanes.

On very busy stretches, there may be overhead gantries with messages about congestion ahead, and a separate signal for each lane. The messages may also give an alternative route which you should use if at all possible.

If you're not sure whether to use the alternative route (for example, can you reach your destination if you use the route suggested), take the next exit, pull over at the first available safe area (lay by or service area) and look at a map.

Remember, on a motorway, once you have passed an exit and encounter congestion, there may not be another opportunity to leave and you could be stuck in slow-moving or stationary traffic for some time. Take the opportunity when it arises, you can always rejoin the motorway if you feel that is the best course of action once you have had time to consider the options.

If you need to change lanes to leave the motorway, do so in good time. At some junctions a lane may lead directly off the motorway. Only get in that lane if you wish to go in the direction indicated on the overhead signs.

Motorway signals can be used to warn you of a danger ahead. For example, there may be an accident, fog, or a spillage, which you may not immediately be able to see.

Amber flashing lights warn of a hazard ahead. The signal may show a temporary maximum speed limit, lanes that are closed or a message such as 'Fog' or 'Q'. Adjust your speed and look out for the danger. Don't increase your speed until you pass a signal which is not flashing or one that gives the 'All clear' sign and you are sure it is safe to increase your speed.

Active Traffic Management

Active Traffic Management (ATM) is a new pilot project to try to reduce congestion and make journey times more reliable.

The pilot scheme will be carried out on a 17 km stretch of the M42 between junctions 3a and 7 in the West Midlands.
ATM will feature benefits including

- close circuit television monitoring every section of this stretch
- high-visibility driver information panels
- new lighting to improve visibility at night and in poor light
- new emergency roadside telephones for use in an emergency or breakdown
- Emergency Refuge Areas for vehicles to use in an emergency or breakdown
- use of the hard-shoulder as an additional running lane under controlled conditions to manage traffic in peak congestion or during an accident
- Highways Agency Traffic Officer patrols monitoring the motorway (see page 135).

Gantries

The new gantries have been built about 500 metres apart on this stretch of motorway. They feature a large message sign board and signal boxes above each of the lanes and the hard shoulder.

Emergency Refuge Areas

These are 100 metres long, wider than the hard-shoulder and are located about every 500 metres. They are designed to be used in cases of emergency or breakdown. Features include

- sensors to alert the control centre that a vehicle has entered
- CCTV enabling the control centre to monitor the vehicles and send assistance as necessary

- new generation Emergency Roadside Telephones containing additional multilingual and hard of hearing support, and the ability to pinpoint your location
- additional distance from the main carriageway.

Driving in actively managed areas

As with driving on any motorway, you must obey the signals displayed on the overhead gantries.

In addition to the normal signals which are used on any motorway (see page 113) there will also be a single red X without flashing beacons which is applicable to the hard shoulder only. When you see this sign, don't use this lane, except in an emergency or breakdown.

There are three driving scenarios

- normal motorway driving conditions
- actively managed mode
- hard-shoulder running mode

Normal Motorway Conditions

- No congestion or incident
- No speed limits shown on signals
- National speed limits apply
- Hard shoulder for emergency and breakdown use only
- Use emergency refuge areas in an emergency for added safety and increased distance from the carriageway
- Use emergency roadside telephone for assistance

Actively Managed Mode

- There may be an incident or congestion ahead
- All speed limit signals are set and must be obeyed
- Driver information panels will provide information for road users
- Red cross over hard shoulder means do not use this lane, except in an emergency or breakdown
- Use emergency refuge areas in an emergency or breakdown for added safety and increased distance from the carriageway
- Use emergency roadside telephone for assistance

Hard Shoulder Running Mode

This is similar to the actively managed mode, except that the hard shoulder may be used as a running lane between junctions. In this case the red cross above the hard shoulder will be replaced by the appropriate speed limit as shown below.

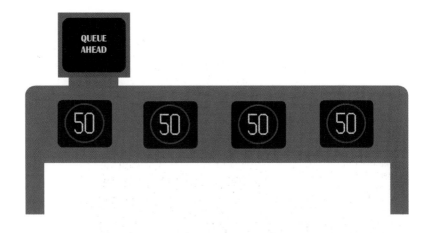

Highways Agency Traffic Officers

Working in partnership with the police, Highways Agency Traffic Officers are extra eyes and ears on the motorways. They are a new, highly-trained and highly-visible service patrolling the motorway to help keep traffic moving and make your journey as safe and reliable as possible.

Traffic Officers wear a full uniform, including a high-visibility orange and yellow jacket, and drive a high-visibility vehicle with yellow and black chequered markings.

Every traffic officer will also have a unique identification number and photographic identity card. They will normally patrol in pairs.

The vehicles contain a variety of equipment for use on the motorway, including temporary road-signs, lights, cones, debris removal tools and a first-aid kit.

Role of a traffic officer

They will

- help broken-down motorists to arrange recovery
- offer safety advice to motorists
- clear debris from the carriageway
- undertake high-visibility patrols
- support the police and emergency services during incidents
- provide mobile/temporary road closures
- manage diversion routes caused by an accident.

If you have an emergency or breakdown on the motorway the best action to take is to use an emergency roadside telephone.

In the West Midlands, emergency roadside telephones are answered by Highways Agency control centre operators located in a regional control centre.

Control centre operators are able to monitor any stranded motorists on close circuit television screens and despatch the nearest available traffic officer patrol to assist.

Powers of traffic officers

Unlike the police, traffic officers will not have any enforcement powers, however they are able to stop and direct anyone travelling on the motorway.

It is an offence not to comply with the directions given by a traffic officer.

Extent of scheme

Initially the scheme started on motorways in the West Midlands but will eventually be extended throughout the English motorway system. By the end of 2005 there will be seven regional control centres in England, managed by the Highways Agency, able to despatch traffic officers to any English motorway.

Traffic Officers will operate on England's motorway network shown here.

Roll out will start in the following areas by:

Current	West Midlands	
Summer 2005	North West and South East	
End of 2005	East, South West, East Midlands, North East	
Legend	Motorway	

Urban Congestion

Congestion in urban areas leads to

- longer journey times
- frustration
- pollution through standing and slow-moving traffic.

London suffers the worst traffic congestion in the UK and amongst the worst in Europe. It has been estimated that

- drivers in central London used to spend 50% of their time in queues
- London lost between £2-4 million every week in terms of lost time caused by congestion.

Various measures have been introduced to try to reduce and alleviate the congestion and make traffic flow more freely. 'Red routes' and 'Congestion charging' are two of the schemes initiated in the London area. These may be introduced into other congested towns and cities.

Red Routes

Red routes keep traffic moving and reduce the pollution that comes from vehicle emissions. Stopping and parking is allowed only within marked boxes.

There is a fixed penalty for an offence and illegally parked vehicles may be towed away.

There are five main types of Red Route markings

Double red lines - stopping is not allowed at any time, for any reason. They are normally placed at road junctions or where parking or loading would be dangerous, or cause serious congestion.

Single red lines - parking, loading or picking up passengers is not allowed during the day (generally 7am to 7pm). Stopping is allowed outside these hours and on Sunday.

Red boxes - indicate parking or loading is permitted during the day at off-peak times, normally 10am to 4pm. Some allow loading and some allow parking, the rules in each case are clearly shown on a sign beside the box.

White boxes - indicate that parking or loading may be allowed at any time, restrictions being clearly shown on the sign beside the box.

Red route clearway - there are no road markings but clearway signs indicate that stopping isn't allowed at any time apart from in marked lay-bys.

Green Issues - helping the environment

The effects of pollution

If you follow the principles of 'Eco-safe driving' set out in the following pages, you will become a more environmentally-friendly driver. Your journeys will be more comfortable and you could considerably reduce both your fuel bills and those emissions that cause damage to the atmosphere.

Developing your planning, perception and anticipation skills will obviously help to make you a safer driver. However, although it's beneficial to save fuel, you mustn't compromise the safety of yourself and other road users when attempting to do so. Road safety is more important. At all times you should be prepared to adapt to changing conditions and it may be that you'll have to sacrifice fuel saving for safety.

What you can do to help

It is still possible to drive a large goods vehicle in a manner more beneficial to the environment by taking a little care and thought to how, and when, you drive. Here are some suggestions on what you can do.

Becoming an Ecosafe Driver

Eco-safe driving is a recognised and proven style of driving that contributes to road safety, whilst reducing fuel consumption and emissions.

One of the main factors in increasing road safety is the emphasis on planning ahead so that you are prepared in advance for potential hazards. By increasing your

hazard perception and planning skills you can make maximum use of your vehicle's momentum and engine braking. By doing this, you can help reduce damage to the environment.

Hazard awareness and planning

You should be constantly scanning all around as you drive. Check into the far distance, midground and foreground, also check behind and to the sides by frequent use of all mirrors. Early recognition of potential hazards is important, but just looking isn't enough, you need to act correctly on what you have seen. This will mean you are able to

- anticipate problems
- take appropriate action in good time to ensure you are travelling at the correct speed when dealing with a hazard.

By doing this you will avoid late braking and harsh acceleration, both of which lead to higher fuel consumption.

Keep a safe distance from the vehicle in front as this will help you to plan your driving. Try to leave yourself sufficient room so you don't always have to brake immediately or harshly when traffic in front of you slows down. By simply taking your foot off the accelerator, your vehicle will slow down and fuel consumption will be reduced. However you may wish to use your brakes to advise vehicles behind that you're slowing down.

If you plan early for hazards you will avoid causing bunching of other road users, traffic will flow more smoothly and you will use less fuel.

Starting up

If your vehicle is fitted with an excess fuel device and you need to use it to start the engine when it's cold, push it in as soon as the engine will run smoothly without it.

Driving away

Avoid over-revving your engine when you start your vehicle and try to pull away smoothly.

Choosing your speed

Always drive sensibly and keep within the speed limit. Exceeding a speed limit by only a few miles per hour will mean that you use more fuel but, more importantly, you are breaking the law and increasing the risk of serious injury if you're involved in a collision.

Use cruise control, when appropriate, if it's fitted. Using cruise control keeps a steady setting on the accelerator so not varying the intake of fuel. It can also help to maintain your speed within the speed limit.

The accelerator

Try to use the accelerator smoothly and progressively. When appropriate, take your foot off the pedal and allow the momentum of the vehicle to take you forward. Taking your foot off the accelerator when going downhill can save a considerable amount of fuel without any loss of vehicle control. Rather than use your brakes for a long period, with the risk of brake fade, you should control downhill speed by use of lower gears.

Whenever possible, avoid rapid acceleration or heavy breaking as this leads to greater fuel consumption and more pollution. Driving smoothly can reduce fuel consumption by about 15% as well as reducing wear and tear on your vehicle.

Selecting gears

It is not always necessary to change up or down through each gear - it is possible to miss out intermediate gears. This helps to reduce the amount of time you spend accelerating, and as this is when fuel consumption is at its highest, you can save fuel by missing out some gears. As soon as conditions allow, use the highest gear possible without making the engine struggle.

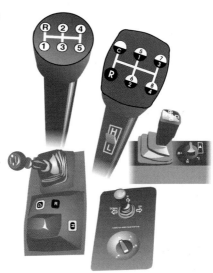

Check your fuel consumption

Check your fuel consumption regularly. To make sure you are getting the most from your vehicle, simply record the amount of fuel you put in against miles travelled. This will help you check whether you're using fuel efficiently.

If you haven't changed your driving method, or the conditions in which you're driving, an increase in the average fuel consumption can mean the vehicle needs servicing. An eco-friendly driver is constantly aware of how much fuel their vehicle uses. If a trip computer is fitted, this can help you check fuel consumption.

Engine braking

With your foot fully off the accelerator the engine needs very little fuel, so take advantage of engine braking wherever possible. Use lower gears rather than extended use of the brakes to avoid brake fade.

Engine power

Modern vehicles are designed to deliver power even when engine revs are quite low. You'll find that you can make use of the higher gears at low speeds.

Route planning

- Plan your route to avoid known hold ups and road works.
- Always know where you're going - you'll use lots of fuel by getting lost.
- If you're likely to be making a prolonged stop, say for more than two minutes at a level crossing or road works, you may consider it best to stop the engine.
- Try to use uncongested routes.

- Make sure you know of any narrow roads or areas where it may be difficult to pass through or manoeuvre a very large vehicle, or where there may be weight, width or height restrictions.
- Try to plan for the easiest way to access your destination.

Continuous research has resulted in new methods of helping the environment by easing traffic flow (see page 130 for advice on avoiding congestion).

Minimising drag

If your vehicle's roof spoiler is adjustable, take it off when not needed, to reduce wind resistance. Spoiler drag can increase fuel consumption by more than 15%.

If it's fitted, use air conditioning only when you need to - running it continuously may increase fuel consumption by about 15%. The alternative to air conditioning may be to open your windows but this will increase drag, and consequently fuel consumption, when you're driving.

Select for economy and low emissions

There are advantages and disadvantages in all types of fuel, however most large goods vehicles are now diesel powered.

These engines are very fuel efficient and produce less carbon dioxide (a global warming gas) than any other road transport fuel. They also emit less carbon monoxide and hydrocarbons than petrol engined vehicles but do produce more emissions of oxides of nigrogen (NOx) and particulates, which are bad for local air quality.

Newer vehicles have to meet strict new emissions standards aimed at reducing these pollutants, and all diesel vehicles can now use ultra-low sulphur diesel fuel to reduce exhaust pollution.

Keep your vehicle well maintained

You should make sure that your vehicle is serviced and maintained regularly.

- Make sure the engine is tuned correctly. Badly-tuned vehicles use more fuel and emit more exhaust fumes. MOT tests now include a strict exhaust emission test to ensure correct tuning, so vehicles operate more efficiently and cause less air pollution.

- Have your vehicle serviced as recommended by the manufacturer. The cost of a service may well be less than the cost of running a badly maintained vehicle - for example, even slight brake drag can increase fuel consumption.

- If you do your own maintenance, make sure that you send oil, old batteries and used tyres to a garage or local authority site for recycling or safe disposal. Don't pour oil down the drain, it's illegal, harmful to the environment and could lead to prosecution.

- Use good quality engine oil - if you use synthetic engine oils rather than the cheaper mineral oil, you can save fuel.

- Make sure your tyres are properly inflated. Incorrect tyre pressure results in shorter tyre life and may create a danger as it can affect stability and braking capacity. In addition, under-inflation can increase fuel consumption and emissions.

RECYCLE USED OIL

When refuelling your vehicle, you should aim to fill it up to the bottom of the filler neck and no further. If you fill the tank to the brim, when the fuel becomes hot and expands, its only way of escape is via the breather vent.

Also, knowing your particular vehicle's average miles or kilometres per gallon (mpg or km/g) can help early identification of problems. If the ratio drops, this may indicate a problem with the vehicle. Drivers are usually the first to notice problems, for example dragging brakes, so here's a checklist of tell tale signs which may indicate that a commercial vehicle needs workshop attention to stop it wasting fuel. Make the following list part of your regular vehicle examination.

Check for

- any fuel or oil leaks
- missing seal in fuel tank cap or signs of fuel spills around filler neck
- low tyre pressure
- tyre wear suggesting faulty steering or axle alignment
- missing tyre valve caps
- traces of black smoke in exhaust
- tears in body curtains/any body damage
- missing/damaged air-management equipment
- excessive engine oil consumption (no leaks) suggestive of internal wear
- maintenance records showing rapid wear of clutch or brake friction material.

Improving fuel economy

Every time you move off, do so smoothly - avoid harsh acceleration.

Change down to the appropriate gear, but wait while speed decreases.

On acceleration, try to skip gears where you can.

Never leave it to chance - maintain your vehicle in good condition.

Observe and keep within the tachometer green zone.

Minimise brake use - plan ahead and keep monitoring road conditions.

Your top speed should remain constant - think "Gear high-rev low'.

Accidents

You should drive at all times with anticipation and awareness. By acting in this way you lessen the risk of being involved in an accident.

It's important to recognise the effects your vehicle can have on more vulnerable road users such as cyclists, pedestrians and motorcyclists. An LGV can create a vacuum effect when travelling at speed. Pedestrians near the edge of the kerb, and cyclists, are especially vulnerable to the danger of being drawn under the wheels of your vehicle or any trailer. You should anticipate at all times the actions of other road users around you. You should

- concentrate
- stay alert
- be fully fit
- observe the changes in traffic conditions
- plan well ahead

- drive at a safe speed to suit the road and traffic conditions
- keep your vehicle in good mechanical condition
- ensure that the load is securely stowed
- drive safely and sensibly
- avoid the need to rush
- don't act hastily.

If your vehicle is involved in a road traffic accident

you must stop.

It's an offence not to do so.

Reporting your accident

It's an offence not to stop if your vehicle is involved in an accident. You must

- produce your insurance documents and driving licence, and give your name and address to any police officer who may require it
- give these details to any other road user involved in the accident if they have reasonable grounds to request them
- if you're unable to produce your documents at the time you must report the accident to the police as soon as possible, or in any case within 24 hours (in Northern Ireland you must report the accident to the police immediately).

You must inform the police as soon as possible, and in any case within 24 hours (you must do this immediately in Northern Ireland), if

- there's injury to any person not in your vehicle
- damage is caused to another vehicle or property and the owner is either not present or can't be found easily
- the accident involves any of the animals specified by law.

The police may require you to produce your documents within seven days at a police station of your choice (five days in Northern Ireland) or as soon as is reasonably possible if you're on a journey that takes you out of the country at the time and you can't produce the documents within the seven days specified.

At the accident scene you must

- exchange particulars with any other driver or road user involved in the accident
- obtain names and addresses of any witnesses who *saw* the accident.

You should make a note of

- the time
- the location
- street names
- vehicle registration numbers
- weather conditions
- lighting (if applicable)
- any road signs or road markings
- road conditions
- damage to vehicles or property
- traffic lights (colour at the time)
- any indicator signals or audible warning given
- any statements made by the other party or parties
- any skid marks, debris, etc.

At an accident scene

If you're the first, or among one of the first, to arrive at the scene of an accident, your actions could be vital. Find a safe place to stop, so you do not endanger yourself, any passengers or other road users. It's essential to

- warn other traffic approaching the scene by means of hazard warning flashers, beacons, cones, advance warning triangles, etc.
- reduce the risk of fire by making sure that all naked lights – cigarettes, etc. – are extinguished
- make sure that someone phones 999, giving details of any injury or danger to other road users
- protect injured persons from any danger from traffic, hazardous materials, etc. It may well be best to keep them still until the emergency services arrive
- be especially careful about moving any casualties – incorrect handling could cause more injury or even prove fatal
- move any apparently uninjured persons away from the vehicle(s) to a place of safety
- give first aid if anyone is unconscious. For advice on first aid, see pages 149-151.
- check for the effects of shock. A person may appear to have no injuries but may be suffering from shock
- keep casualties warm but give them nothing to drink
- give the *facts* (not assumptions, etc.) to the ambulance crew when they arrive.

Do not remove a motorcyclist's helmet unless it is essential to do so.

Accidents on the motorway

Because of the higher speeds on motorways and increased danger of an accident becoming a serious incident, it's essential to inform the motorway police and emergency services as quickly as possible.

You should

- use the nearest emergency telephone – it is free and connects directly to the police. If you use a mobile telephone, first make sure you have identified your location
- not cross the carriageway to get to an emergency telephone
- try to warn traffic behind, if possible, without placing yourself in danger
- move any uninjured people well away from the main carriageway and onto an embankment, etc.
- be on the alert for emergency vehicles approaching the incident along the hard shoulder.

Emergency vehicles

Be aware that emergency vehicles may approach at any time while you are on the road. You should look and listen for flashing blue, red or green lights, headlights or sirens being used by ambulances, fire engines, police or other emergency vehicles. When one approaches do not panic; consider the route it is taking and take appropriate action to let it pass. If necessary, pull to the side of the road and stop, but make sure you are aware of other road users and that you do not endanger them in any way.

If you see or hear emergency vehicles in the distance, be aware that there may be an accident ahead and that other emergency vehicles may be approaching.

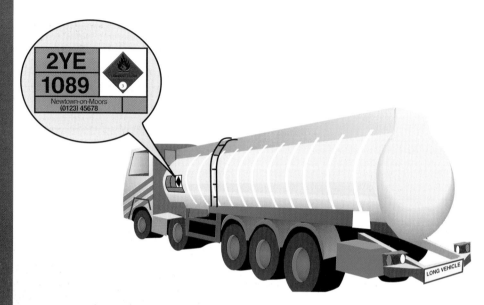

Dangerous goods

If a road traffic accident involves a vehicle displaying either a hazard warning information plate or a plain orange rectangle

- give the emergency services as much information as possible about the labels and any other markings
- contact the emergency telephone number on the plate of a vehicle involved in any spillage, if a number is given
- do not use a mobile phone close to a vehicle carrying flammable loads
- keep well away from such a vehicle unless you have to save a life

- beware of any dangerous liquids, dusts or vapours – no matter how small the concentration may appear to be. People have received extremely serious injuries as a result of a fine spray of corrosive fluid leaking from a pinhole puncture in a tank vessel.

Examples of various hazard labels are shown on page 236.

Fire

Fire can occur on LGVs in a number of locations, for example

- engine
- load
- transmission
- tyres
- fuel system
- electrical circuits.

It's vital that any fire is tackled without delay. A vehicle and its load can be destroyed by fire within an alarmingly short period of time.

If fire is suspected or discovered, in order to avoid danger to others it's essential to

- stop as quickly and safely as possible
- get all individuals out of the vehicle
- either dial 999 or get someone else to do it immediately

Carrying a suitable fire extinguisher in your vehicle may help you to put out a small fire. If you suspect a fire in the engine compartment, take the actions shown in the three bullet points above but also

- DO NOT open the bonnet
- You may be able to direct any available fire extinguisher nozzle through the small gap available when the release catch is operated
- If the fire appears to be large DO NOT try to tackle it, get well clear of the vehicle and leave it to the fire brigade
- DO NOT take any risks.

If the fire involves a vehicle carrying dangerous goods

- the driver must have received training in dealing with such an emergency
- specialist fire-fighting equipment must be available on the vehicle.

You should

- keep all members of the public and other traffic well away from the incident
- isolate the vehicle to reduce danger to the surrounding area
- ensure that someone contacts, without delay, the emergency telephone number given on either the hazard warning plate or the load documents
- warn approaching traffic.

Stay calm

React promptly

Old-style UK fire extinguishers

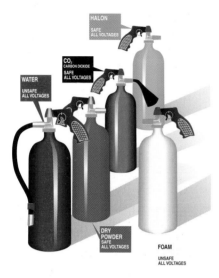

Fire extinguishers

You should be able to recognise the various types of fire extinguisher and know which fires they're intended to tackle. For example, it's dangerous to tackle a fuel fire with a water or carbon dioxide fire extinguisher, since this may only spread the fire further.

Most extinguishers are intended to smother the source of the fire by either the action of an inert gas or a dry powder. Try to isolate the source of the fire. If at all possible

- disconnect electrical leads
- cut off the fuel supply.

Don't open an engine housing wide if you can direct the extinguisher through a small gap. Also, avoid operating a fire extinguisher in a confined space.

Vehicles carrying dangerous goods and other materials which may pose a hazard are subject to detailed emergency procedures which must be followed. Never

put yourself in danger when tackling a fire. Always call the fire service as quickly as possible because they are the experts. Make sure any passengers leave the vehicle and go to a place of safety.

*Note

Halon fire extinguishers may still be used. However, halon is no longer manufactured in the EU for environmental reasons. Once used, a halon extinguisher cannot be refilled and should be replaced with a suitable alternative, such as a dry powder extinguisher.

New-style UK fire extinguishers

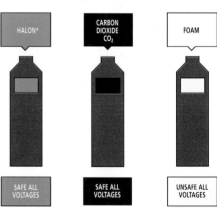

First aid

Regulations require many LGVs carrying chemicals, etc., to carry first aid equipment. Even if you don't have to carry a kit by law, it's sensible for every LGV driver to have a first aid kit available.

You should really consider doing first aid training. One day it could save a life. There are courses available from the

- St John Ambulance Association and Brigade
- St Andrew's Ambulance Association
- British Red Cross Society.

The following information may be of some assistance, but it is no substitute for proper training.

First aid on the road

Any first aid given at the scene of an accident should only be looked on as a temporary measure until the emergency services arrive. If you haven't any training the following points could be helpful.

Accident victims

It is essential that the following are given immediate priority if the casualty is unconscious and permanent injury is to be avoided.

Remember the letters ABC

- *A* – the airway must be cleared and kept open
- *B* – breathing must be established and maintained
- *C* – blood circulation must be maintained and severe bleeding stopped.

Airways   Check for and relieve any obstruction to breathing. Unless you suspect head or neck injury, remove any obvious obstruction in the mouth (false teeth, chewing gum, etc.)

Breathing   Breathing should begin and colour improve. If there's no improvement after the airway has been cleared

- tilt the head back very gently
- place a clean piece of material, such as a handkerchief, over the injured person's mouth
- pinch the casualty's nostrils together
- blow into the mouth until the chest rises. Take your mouth away and wait for the chest to fall
- repeat regularly once every four seconds until the casualty can breathe without help.

With babies and small children

- let your mouth surround their mouth and nose and breathe very gently
- take your mouth away and wait for the chest to fall
- withdraw, then repeat regularly once every four seconds until breathing restarts and the casualty can breathe without help.

Don't give up!

Never assume someone is dead. Keep giving mouth-to-mouth resuscitation until medical help is available.

Circulation   Prevent blood loss to maintain circulation. If bleeding is present, follow the procedure on page 150 to stem it.

Unconscious and breathing

Do not move a casualty unless there's further danger. Movement could add to spinal/neck injury. If breathing is difficult or stops, treat as recommended in the breathing section. Don't attempt to remove a motorcyclist's safety helmet unless it's essential – otherwise serious injury could result.

Bleeding

To stem the flow of blood put firm pressure on the wound without pressing on anything that may be caught in or projecting from the wound.

As soon as practicable secure a pad to the wound with a bandage or length of cloth. Use the cleanest material available.

If a limb is bleeding, but not broken, raise it to lessen the flow of blood. Any restriction of blood circulation for more than a short period of time may result in long-term injuries.

It's vital to obtain skilled medical help as soon as possible. Make sure that someone dials 999.

Burns

Check the casualty for shock, and if possible, try to cool the burn. Try to find a liquid that is clean, cold and non-toxic with which to douse it.

Do not try to remove anything which is stuck to the burn.

Dealing with shock

The effects of trauma may not be immediately obvious.

Warning signs to look for include

- rapid pulse
- pale grey skin
- sweating
- rapid, shallow breathing.

Prompt treatment can help to minimise the effects of shock. You should

- reassure the victim confidently and keep checking them
- keep any casualties warm and make them as comfortable as possible
- try to calm a hysterical person by talking to them in firm, quiet tones
- make sure that shock victims don't run into further danger from traffic
- avoid leaving the casualty alone
- avoid unnecessary movement of a casualty
- if a casualty does need to be moved for their own safety, take care to avoid making their injuries worse.

You should not

- give victims anything to drink until medical advice is available.

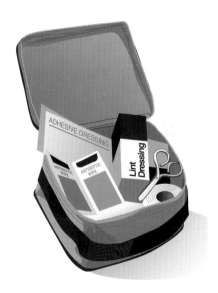

Electric shock

A vehicle can come into contact with overhead cables or electrical supplies to traffic bollards, traffic lights or street lighting standards as a result of an accident. Make a quick check before attempting to pull someone from a vehicle in such cases.

Don't touch any person who is obviously in contact with a live electric cable unless you can use some non-conducting item, such as a length of **dry** wood, plastic or similar - nothing wet should be used. You **must not** try to give first aid until contact has been broken.

A person can also be electrocuted by simply being too close to a high voltage overhead cable. Contact the provider, a number may be shown on a nearby pole, then follow their advice.

Breakdowns

Tyre failures

Many LGV breakdowns involve tyre failures or 'blow-outs'. Not only are these dangerous in themselves, by causing loss of control, but the resulting debris also presents a common hazard to other road users.

Front wheel blow-outs

A sudden deflation of the front tyre on an LGV can result in a loss of steering control. You should

- keep firm hold of the steering wheel
- always be aware of anything on your nearside
- signal to move to the left
- try to steer a steady course to the nearside (or hard shoulder on the motorway)
- reduce speed gradually and avoid any harsh braking
- try to bring the vehicle to rest under control and as far to the left as possible
- use a warning triangle, if you have one. Place it behind the vehicle and operate the hazard flashers if the vehicle is causing an obstruction
- avoid sharp braking and excessive steering movements. You should be able to bring the vehicle to rest safely by reducing the risk of skidding.

Rear wheel blow-outs

If a rear tyre on either the vehicle or a trailer deflates the effects may not be quite so severe. On a large vehicle this may not be immediately obvious to you, especially if it's a multi-axle trailer. Keep the trailer under observation at all times during a journey.

Lost wheels

Regular maintenance is essential to help prevent wheels becoming detached during use. When the wheels have been removed and replaced for any reason, it's important to re-check the wheel nuts shortly after their initial tightening. Check the wheel fixings regularly during use, preferably as part of your inspection routine prior to starting any journey.

It's essential that wheel fixings are tightened to the torque specified by the vehicle manufacturer. You should also use a torque wrench that's frequently calibrated.

Further information is given in the British Standard Code of Practice for the selection and care of tyres and wheels for commercial vehicles. This has been developed with the support and involvement of the major transport operators' associations. The relevant reference number is BS AU 50: Part 2: Section 7a: 1995, and it's available from

British Standards Institution
389 Chiswick High Road
London W4 4AL.

Tel: 020 8996 9000

Website: www.bsi-global.com

Part Five

Preparing for the driving test

The topics covered

- About the driving test
- The theory test
- How to apply for your test
- Before attending your test
- Legal requirements
- At the test centre
- The official syllabus

About the driving test

When taking the LGV practical driving test you should aim for a professional standard. You'll pass if your examiner sees that you can

- drive safely to a high standard
- show expert handling of the controls
- carry out the set exercises accurately and under control
- demonstrate through your driving that you have a thorough knowledge of *The Highway Code* and other matters concerning vehicle safety.

Does the standard of the test vary?

No. All examiners are trained to carry out the test to the same standard. Test routes

- are as uniform as possible
- include a wide range of typical road and traffic conditions.

You should have the same results from different examiners or at different LGV driving test centres.

How your driving test is assessed

Your examiner will assess any errors you make. They will be assessed and recorded depending on their degree of seriousness and marked on the Driving Test Report form (DLV25).

You will fail your test if you commit a serious or dangerous fault. You will also fail if you accumulate too many driving faults (previously known as minor faults).

The criteria the examiner will use are as follows

Driving fault – less serious but has been assessed as such because of circumstances at that particular time.

Serious fault – recorded when a potentially dangerous incident has occurred or a habitual driving fault indicates a serious weakness in a candidate's driving.

Dangerous fault – recorded when a fault is assessed as having caused actual danger during the test.

At the end of the test you will be offered some general guidance to explain your driving test report.

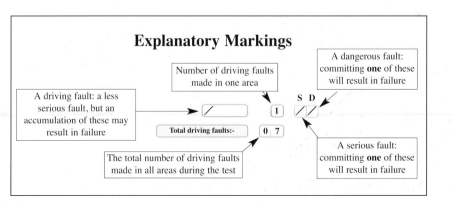

Explanatory Markings

Number of driving faults made in one area

A dangerous fault: committing **one** of these will result in failure

A driving fault: a less serious fault, but an accumulation of these may result in failure

Total driving faults:-

A serious fault: committing **one** of these will result in failure

The total number of driving faults made in all areas during the test

Are examiners supervised?

Yes, they're closely supervised. A senior officer may sit in on your test if there are two or more passenger seats in your vehicle.

Don't worry about this. The supervising officer won't be examining you, but will be checking that the examiner is carrying out the test properly. Just carry on as if she or he wasn't there.

Can anyone accompany me on the test?

Due to lack of seats this isn't always possible. If there are three or more seats in the cab of your vehicle, and provided a DSA supervisor isn't intending to observe the test, your instructor is allowed to be present, but can't take any part in the test.

How should I drive during the test?

Drive in the way that your instructor has taught you. If you make a mistake, try not to worry. It might be minor and may not affect the result of the test. Your examiner will be looking for a high overall standard. Don't worry about one or two minor mistakes.

What will my examiner want from me?

Your examiner will want you to drive safely to a high standard under various road and traffic conditions. You'll be

- given directions clearly and in good time
- asked to carry out set exercises.

Due to the higher level of engine noise in the cab your examiner will make sure that you're able to hear the directions clearly.

Your examiner will be understanding and sympathetic. They will try to put you at your ease to help you to do your best.

What will the test consist of?

Apart from general driving, the test will include

- reversing within a marked area into a restricted opening
- a braking exercise
- a gear-changing exercise, if you're driving a manual vehicle
- moving off on the level, at an angle, uphill and downhill
- demonstrating the uncoupling and recoupling procedure, if you're taking your test with a trailer.

You will also need to satisfy the examiner that you're capable of preparing to drive safely by carrying out simple safety checks on the vehicle you're using on the test.

Some of these exercises are always carried out at the test centre. These are the

- safety check questions
- reversing exercise
- braking exercise
- uncoupling and recoupling exercise.

The rest of the exercises will take place during the road section of the test.

During the reversing exercise your examiner will remain outside the vehicle.

Your examiner will join you in the cab before explaining the braking exercise to you. They will watch your handling of the controls as you carry out the exercise.

This exercise will be carried out before you leave the test centre. If your vehicle doesn't pull up satisfactorily your examiner may decide not to continue the test, in the interest of safety.

What if I don't understand?

Your examiner will be as helpful as possible and will explain what's required. Before the exercises you'll be shown a diagram. This will make it easier to understand what's required. You'll then be asked to carry out the exercise. If you aren't sure, ask. Your examiner won't mind explaining again.

How long will the test last?

About 90 minutes.

When will I be ready for my test?

When you've reached the standards set in this book – not before. You should ensure that you receive good instruction, together with as much practice as you can.

How will I know when I'm ready?

You're ready for your practical test when you're driving

- consistently well
- with confidence
- in complete control
- without assistance and guidance from your instructor.

Most people fail because they haven't had enough instruction and practice. Make sure that all aspects of the syllabus for learning to drive an LGV are covered (see pages 165 - 175).

Special circumstances

You'll have had to pass a medical in order to obtain your provisional licence. Your doctor will have had to declare if there's any reason why you wouldn't have full control of a large vehicle. There may be circumstances when adaptations to a vehicle may overcome a particular disability.

To make sure that enough time is allowed for your test it would help DSA to know

- if you're restricted in any way in your movements
- if you have any disability that might affect your driving.

Please include this information when you apply for your test.

Your examiner may wish to talk to you about your disability and any adaptations you may have fitted to your vehicle.

Language difficulties

If you have difficulty speaking or understanding English, you can bring an interpreter with you. Remember, the vehicle must have enough seats. The interpreter must be 16 years or over and must not be your instructor.

The theory test

Before you take your practical LGV driving test you'll have to pass an LGV theory test. You must satisfy your examiner that you've **fully understood** everything that you learned for the theory test.

The various aspects include the knowledge of

- the height, weight, width and length of your vehicle. This enables you to drive on roads with a full knowledge of any restrictions that might apply to your vehicle

- rules on drivers' hours and rest periods, so that you can obey the legal requirements and are fit to drive safely

- braking systems and speed limiters. You should be fully aware of how your brakes work and the importance of using them effectively

- the restricted view you have around your vehicle due to its size and dimensions. This size will also affect other road users' view – you must be aware of this

- faults on your vehicle and being able to recognise and report any defects

- the factors relating to loading a vehicle safely and securely

- the effect of wind on your vehicle and on other road users around you

- the dangers of splashing spray or mud on other road users when overtaking them

- the course you have to take when turning, in order to allow for the length or overhang of your vehicle

- the correct actions to take if you're involved in or arrive at an accident

- reducing the risks when overtaking other road users

- the dangers of leaving the cab of your vehicle on the offside.

As well as the multiple choice questions, the theory test now includes a hazard perception part. To prepare for this DSA strongly recommends that you study and work through the hazard perception training material. The DVD is entitled *The official guide to hazard perception* and there is also a video and workbook-based training pack called *Roadsense*.

If you've passed your LGV theory test you'll have shown that you've taken the time to learn the basic aspects of becoming an LGV driver.

At the start of the drive in your practical test your examiner will ask you to follow the road ahead, unless asked to turn or traffic signs direct you otherwise. From this point you should be able to demonstrate your understanding of the topics covered in the theory test.

How to apply for your test

You must have a provisional licence for the category of vehicle that you're going to drive.

Booking online or by phone

You can book your theory and practical tests on the DSA Website or by telephone using a credit or debit card. Most major credit and debit cards are accepted. You must be the card holder; if you aren't then the card holder must be present.

For information about fees and to book a test, phone 0870 01 01 372.

The booking clerk will want to know

- your driver number, shown on your licence
- the type of test you wish to book
- your personal details (name, address, day/evening telephone numbers)
- unacceptable days or periods
- any special circumstances, such as being accompanied by an interpreter
- your credit card number and expiry date (and the issue number when using Switch).

If you are booking your practical test you will need to provide your theory test certificate number.

If you use either of these services, you will be offered a date and time for your test immediately. You will be given a booking number and sent an appointment within a few days.

The application form

You can obtain an application form (DLV26) from a DSA LGV/PCV driving test centre. Look at the guidance notes carefully, especially those that refer to vehicle categories.

Make sure that you give all the particulars asked for on the application form. If you miss anything out it could delay the date of your test.

Don't forget to send your fee. You may do this by sending a cheque or postal order. Make sure that it's crossed and made payable to the Driving Standards Agency. If you send a postal order keep the counterfoil.

Please don't send cash

Send your application form to

DSA
PO Box 280
Newcastle-Upon Tyne
NE99 1FP

Trainer booking

If you're learning to drive with a training organisation they'll normally book your test for you. An arrangement with the Area Office allows them to book and pay for test appointments in advance. This enables them to arrange courses to culminate with a test appointment.

If you're a trainer and are interested in this scheme contact DSA's booking section: 0870 01 01 372.

Visit the website

More information and guidance on all aspects of booking or taking a driving test can be found on the DSA website at **www.driving-tests.co.uk.**

Saturday and evening tests

Saturday and weekday evening tests are available at some driving test centres. The fees for these are higher than for a driving test during the normal working hours on weekdays.

Evening tests are available during the summer months only.

You can get details from

- DSA national booking number: 0870 01 01 372
- driving test centres
- your instructor.

Your test appointment

The DSA will send you a notification of your appointment, which is the receipt of your fee. Take this with you when you attend your test. The notification will include

- the time and place of your test
- the address of the driving test centre
- other important information.

If you haven't received notification after two weeks contact the national booking number 0870 01 01 372.

Postponing your test

Contact the DSA national booking number if

- the date or time of your appointment isn't suitable
- you want to postpone or cancel your test.

There's a cancellation date on your appointment card. If you wish to cancel your test you should do so before this date or you'll lose your fee.

Before attending your test

Documents

You must have applied for and received a provisional licence for the category in which you wish to take your test. Make sure that you have your provisional driving licence and your theory test pass certificate with you. Photocopies are not acceptable. Check that you've signed your licence – your test might be cancelled if you haven't done this.

If you have a photo licence you must bring both parts of the licence (photocard and paper counterpart) to the test.

Photographic identification

If your licence does not show your photograph you must also bring with you a form of photographic identification. For this your examiner will accept

- a signed passport or document of like nature. The passport does not have to be a British one.

or any of the following identification cards, provided it shows your photograph and your signature

- an employer's identity or workplace pass
- trades union card or students' union membership card
- card for the purchase of reduced price rail tickets
- cheque guarantee card or credit card
- gun licence

If you don't have any of these you can bring a photograph, together with a statement that it's a true likeness of you. A signature will be accepted from the following

- LGV instructor who is included on the DSA register of approved LGV instructors

- Approved Driving Instructor (not a trainee)
- DSA certified motorcycle instructor
- Member of Parliament
- medical practitioner
- local authority councillor
- teacher (qualified)
- Justice of the Peace
- civil servant (established)
- police officer
- bank official
- minister of religion
- barrister or solicitor
- Commissioned Officer in Her Majesty's Forces.

I ....
(name of certifier), certify that this is a
true likeness of ....
who has been known to me for ....
(number) months/years in my capacity as
....
Signed ....
Date ....

If you don't bring these documents with you on the day you won't be able to take your test and you will lose your fee. If you have any queries about what photographic evidence we will accept, contact the national enquiry line.

No photo

No licence

No test

Legal requirements

Your test vehicle

Make sure that the vehicle you intend to drive

- is legally roadworthy and has a current certificate issued by the Vehicle Inspectorate
- is fully covered by insurance for its present use and for you to drive
- is unladen and doesn't have any large advertising boards fixed to the flat bed of the vehicle
- is in the category in which you want to hold a licence
- has ordinary L plates visible to the front and rear (or D plates, if you wish, when driving in Wales)
- has a seat in the cab for the examiner
- has enough fuel, not only for the test (at least 20 miles) but also for you to return to base
- isn't being used on a trade licence.

Test vehicles in all categories must be fitted with an anti-lock braking system and a tachograph.

You should also check the vehicle's

- stop lamps
- direction indicators
- lenses and reflectors
- mirrors
- brakes
- tyres
- exhaust system (for excessive noise)
- windscreen and washers
- wipers.

Make sure that the cab is clean and free from any loose equipment.

Change of vehicle

Please let the Area Office know if you want to bring a different vehicle from the one described on your application form. This will avoid unnecessary delay when you arrive for your test.

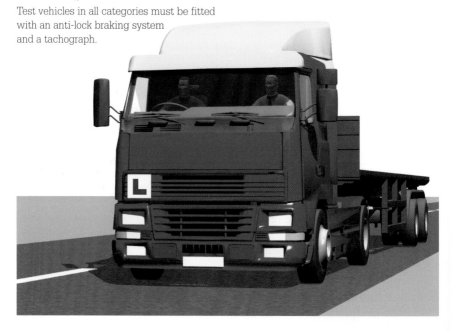

Minimum test vehicles (MTVs)

For full details of minimum test vehicle requirements, see pages 230-231.

Other legal requirements

You must show that you're competent to drive the vehicle in which the test is being conducted without danger to, and with due consideration for, other persons on the road. The legal requirements state that you must be able to

- start the engine
- move off straight and at an angle
- maintain a proper position in relation to other vehicles
- overtake and take an appropriate course in relation to other vehicles
- turn left and right
- stop within a limited distance, under full control
- stop normally and bring the vehicle to a rest in an appropriate part of the road

- drive the vehicle forward and backward, and whilst driving the vehicle backward steer it along a permitted course so that it enters a restricted opening and then bring it to rest in a predetermined position
- indicate your intended actions by appropriate signals at appropriate times
- act correctly and promptly in response to all signals given by any traffic sign, any person lawfully directing traffic or any other person using the road
- uncouple and recouple your trailer (if appropriate).

Your examiner won't carry out an eyesight test at the beginning of the practical test. You should already have met the requirements before your provisional licence was issued.

At the test centre

Before the drive

Make sure that you arrive in good time. The test will take about 90 minutes, so you need to ensure that you won't exceed the number of hours that you're allowed to drive by law.

Your examiner will call your name and ask to see your licence and photo ID, and, if appropriate, your theory test pass certificate. Make sure that you've signed your licence. She or he will then ask you to sign a declaration that your insurance is in order. The test won't be conducted if you're unable to do so. When you've done this you'll be asked to lead the way to your vehicle.

Your vehicle will have been left unattended so walk around it and make a visual check of

- lights
- tyres
- number plate
- couplings (if appropriate)
- cab locking mechanism (if fitted).

Before you start the engine you must always check that

- all doors are properly closed
- your seat is properly adjusted and comfortable so that you can reach all the controls easily
- you have good all-round vision

Declaration

I declare that my use of the test vehicle for the purposes of the test is covered by a valid policy of insurance which satisfies the requirements of the relevant legislation

SIGNED

- your driving mirrors are properly adjusted
- if fitted, your seat belt is fastened, correctly adjusted and comfortable
- the handbrake is on
- the gear lever is in neutral.

Develop this routine while you're learning.

Once you've started the engine, if your vehicle is fitted with air brakes wait until the gauges show the correct pressure, or until any device (a buzzer sounding or a light flashing) has stopped operating.

The official syllabus

As the driver of a large vehicle you must make safety your first priority – not just your own safety, but also that of other road users. The information in this book describes and encourages the safe driving techniques you should put into practice.

Driving in itself is a life skill, but when considering driving an LGV it's also the means by which you earn your living. It may take many years to gain the skills set out here, but you'll need to aim for professional standards right from the very start.

Whether you learn with an instructor or as 'work experience' with a colleague, you must be satisfied that you've fully covered all aspects of the officially recommended syllabus. You may find it helpful to check your progress against the actual syllabus requirements, so they're given here in full.

This syllabus lists the skills that you must have in order to reach the high standards required to pass the LGV driving test and to become a professional lorry driver. It's impossible to give details of all the rules and regulations that apply to both the driver and their vehicle in a book of this size. However, you'll need to know and keep up to date with current requirements.

You must have a thorough knowledge of

- the latest edition of *The Highway Code,* especially those sections that concern lorries
- regulations governing drivers' permitted hours
- regulations relating to the carriage of hazardous and other specialised goods.

You must also have a thorough understanding of general motoring regulations, especially

- road traffic offences
- licences, both drivers' and operators', where applicable
- insurance requirements
- vehicle road tax relating to LGVs (and any trailer) in your charge
- plating of LGVs and their trailers
- annual testing of LGVs.

Legal requirements

To learn to drive an LGV you must

1. Normally be at least 21 years old.
2. Meet the stringent eyesight requirements.
3. Be medically fit to drive lorries.
4. Hold a full car licence (category B).
5. Hold and comply with the conditions for holding a provisional licence in the category of LGV being driven.
6. Hold a full licence in category C and a provisional licence for C + E if driving a vehicle in that category.

7. Ensure that the vehicle being driven
   - is legally roadworthy
   - is correctly plated
   - has a current test certificate (MOT)
   - is properly licensed with the correct tax disc displayed.
8. Make sure that the vehicle being driven is properly insured for its use, especially if it's on contract hire.
9. Display L plates to the front and rear of the vehicle (D plates, if you wish, when driving in Wales).
10. Be accompanied by a supervisor who holds a valid full licence for the category of vehicle being driven.
11. Wear a seat belt, if fitted, unless you're exempt. Ensure that all seat belts in the vehicle, and their anchorages and fittings, are secure and free from obvious defects.

    Children shouldn't normally be carried in LGVs. However, if a child is carried in the vehicle, with permission, you must comply with all regulations relating to the wearing of seat belts by children or the use of child restraints.
12. Be aware that it's a legal requirement to notify the DVLA of any medical condition that could affect safe driving if the period for which you are affected is likely to be three months or more.
13. Ensure that any adaptations are suitable to control the vehicle safely if the vehicle has been adapted for any disability.

Vehicle controls, equipment and components

You must

1. Understand the function of the
   - accelerator
   - clutch
   - gears
   - footbrake
   - handbrake
   - secondary brake
   - steering

   and be able to use these competently.

2. Know the function of all other controls and switches on the vehicle and be able to use them competently.

3. Understand the meanings of
   - gauges
   - warning lights
   - warning buzzers
   - other displays on the instrument panel.

4. Be familiar with the operation of tachographs and their charts.

5. Know the legal requirements that apply to the vehicle's
   - speed limits
   - weight limits
   - braking system (ABS)
   - fire extinguishers to be carried.

6. Know how to carry out routine safety checks, and identify defects, especially on the
   - power steering
   - brakes (tractor unit + semi-trailer on articulated, or rigid vehicle + trailer on combinations)
   - air pressure in the air tanks
   - suspension
   - wheels, wheelnuts and mudguards
   - tyres on all wheels
   - seat belts
   - lights
   - reflectors/reflective plates
   - direction indicators
   - marker lights
   - windscreen, wipers and washers
   - horn
   - rear view mirrors
   - speedometer
   - instruments including tachograph
   - exhaust system
   - brake line and electrical connections on rigid vehicles + trailers, or articulated vehicles
   - coupling gear
   - hydraulic and lubricating systems
   - self-loading or tailgate equipment
   - drop-side hinges and tailgate fastenings
   - curtain-side fittings/fastenings
   - winches or auxiliary gear, where these items are fitted.

7. Know the safety factors relating to
   - stowage
   - loading
   - stability
   - restraint

   of any load carried on the vehicle.

8. Know the effects speed limiters will have on the control of your vehicle, especially when you intend to overtake.

9. Know the principles of the various systems of retarders that may be fitted to LGVs including
   - electric
   - engine-driven
   - exhaust brakes

   and when they should be brought into operation.

Road user behaviour

You must

1. Know the most common causes of road traffic accidents.

2. Know which road users are more vulnerable and how to reduce the risks to them.

3. Know the rules, risks and effects of drinking and driving.

4. Know the effects that
   - illness (even minor ones)
   - drugs or cold remedies
   - tiredness

   can have on driving performance.

5. Recognise the importance of complying with rest period regulations.

6. Be aware of the age-dependent problems among other road users including
   - children
   - young cyclists
   - young drivers
   - more elderly drivers
   - elderly or infirm pedestrians

7. Concentrate and plan ahead in order to anticipate the likely actions of other road users and be able to select the safest course of action.

Vehicle characteristics

You must

1. Know the most important principles concerning braking distances under various
   - road
   - weather
   - loading

   conditions.

2. Know the different handling characteristics of other vehicles with regard to
   - speed
   - stability
   - braking
   - manoeuvrability.

3. Know that some other vehicles, such as bicycles and motorcycles, are less easily seen than others.

4. Be aware of the difficulties caused by the characteristics of both your own and other vehicles, and be able to take the appropriate action to reduce any risks that might arise.

Examples are

- LGVs and buses moving to the right before making a sharp left turn
- drivers of articulated vehicles having to take what appears to be an incorrect line before negotiating corners, roundabouts or entrances
- blind spots that occur on many large vehicles
- bicycles, motorcycles and high-sided vehicles being buffeted in strong winds, especially on exposed sections of road
- turbulence created by LGVs travelling at speed, affecting pedestrians, cyclists, motorcyclists, vehicles towing caravans, and drivers of smaller motor vehicles.

At all times, remember that other road users may not understand the techniques required to manoeuvre an LGV safely.

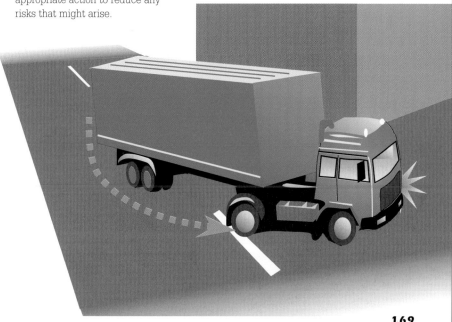

Road and weather conditions

You must

1. Know the various hazards that can arise when driving
   - in strong sunlight
   - at dusk or dawn
   - during the hours of darkness
   - on various types of road such as
     - country lanes in rural areas
     - one-way streets
     - two-way roads in built-up areas
     - three-lane roads
     - dual carriageways with various speed limits
     - trunk roads with two-way traffic
     - motorways.

2. Gain experience in driving on urban roads with 20 or 30 mph speed limits, and also on roads carrying dense traffic volumes at higher speed limits in both daylight and during the hours of darkness.

3. Gain experience in driving on both urban and rural motorways.

4. Know which road surfaces will provide better or poorer grip when braking.

5. Know all the associated hazards caused by bad weather such as
   - rain
   - snow
   - ice
   - fog.

6. Be able to assess the difficulties caused by
   - road
   - traffic
   - weather

   conditions.

7. Drive professionally and anticipate how the prevailing conditions may affect the standard of driving shown by other road users.

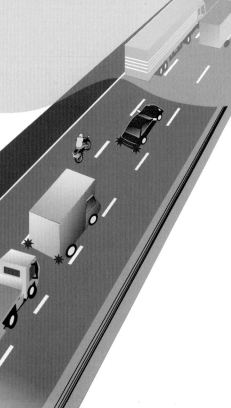

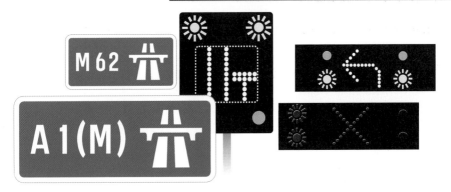

Traffic signs, rules and regulations

You must

1. Have a thorough knowledge and understanding of the meanings of traffic signs and road markings.

2. Be able to recognise and comply with traffic signs that indicate

   - weight limits
   - height limits
   - when LGVs are prohibited
   - loading/unloading restrictions
   - traffic calming measures
     - 20 mph zones
     - road width restrictions
     - speed-reduction humps
   - roads designated Red Routes
   - night-time and weekend lorry bans such as those used in the London boroughs.

Vehicle control and road procedure

You must have the knowledge and skill to carry out safely and expertly the following list of tasks (when appropriate) in daylight and, if necessary, during the hours of darkness. Where the tasks involve other road users you must

- make proper use of the mirrors
- take effective observation
- give signals where necessary.

1. Take the following necessary precautions, where they're applicable, before getting into the vehicle

   - ensure that number plates are correct and securely fitted
   - check all round for obstructions
   - ensure that any load is secure
   - check that air lines are correctly fitted and free from leaks
   - check all couplings to the drawing vehicle and trailer
   - check that the landing gear is raised
   - check that the trailer brake is released
   - check that all bulbs, lenses and reflectors are fitted.
   - make sure that all lights, indicators and stop lights are working
   - ensure that all reflective plates are visible, clean and secure
   - examine tyres for defects
   - examine all load restraints for tension, etc.
   - ensure that any unused ropes are safely stowed.

2. Before leaving the vehicle cab make sure that

- the vehicle is stopped in a safe, legal and secure place
- the handbrake is on
- the engine is stopped
- the electrical system is switched off
- the gear lever/selector is in neutral
- all windows are closed
- the passenger door is secure
- the keys have been removed from the starter switch
- you won't endanger anyone when you open the door.

3. Before starting the engine carry out the following safety checks

- handbrake is applied
- gear lever is in neutral
- doors are properly closed
- your seat is adjusted for
  - height
  - distance from the controls
  - back rest support and comfort
- the mirrors are correctly adjusted
- your seat belt is fastened and adjusted.

4. Start the engine, but before moving off check that

- the vehicle (and any trailer) lights are on, if required
- gauges indicate correct pressures for the braking system
- no warning lights are showing
- no warning buzzer is operating
- no ABS fault indicator is lit (where fitted)
- all fuel and temperature gauges are operating normally
- engine pre-heater lamp (glow plug) is operating (where fitted)
- it's safe to move off by looking all round, especially in the blind spots.

5. Move off

- straight ahead
- at an angle
- on the level
- uphill
- downhill.

6. Select the correct road position for normal driving.

7. Practise effective observation in all traffic conditions.

8. Drive at a speed appropriate to the road, traffic and weather conditions.

9. Anticipate changes in traffic conditions and adopt the correct action at all times and exercise vehicle sympathy.

10. Move into the appropriate traffic lane correctly and in good time.

11. Pass stationary vehicles safely.

12. Meet, overtake and cross the path of other vehicles safely.

13. Turn right or left at
    – junctions
    – crossroads
    – roundabouts.

14. Drive ahead at crossroads and roundabouts.

15. Keep a safe separation gap when following other vehicles.

16. Act correctly at all types of pedestrian crossing.

17. Show proper regard for the safety of all other road users, with particular respect for those most vulnerable.

18. Drive on
    – urban roads
    – rural roads
    – dual carriageways

    keeping up with the traffic flow (but still observing speed limits) where it's safe and appropriate to do so.

19. Comply with
    – traffic regulations
    – traffic signs
    – signals given by authorised persons
    – police officers.

20. Take the correct action on signals given by other road users.

21. Stop the vehicle safely at all times.

22. Select safe and suitable places to stop the vehicle, when requested, reasonably close to the nearside kerb
    – on the level
    – facing uphill
    – facing downhill
    – before reaching a parked vehicle, but leaving sufficient room to move away again.

23. Stop the vehicle on the braking exercise manoeuvring area
    – safely
    – as quickly as possible
    – under full control
    – within a reasonable distance from a designated point.

24. Reverse the vehicle on the manoeuvring area
    – under control
    – with effective observation
    – on a predetermined course
    – to enter a restricted opening
    – to stop with the extreme rear of the vehicle within a clearly defined area.

25. Cross all types of level crossings
    – railway
    – rapid transit systems (trams)
    where appropriate.

26. Uncouple and recouple the tractor unit and trailer. When uncoupling you must

 – select a place with safe and level ground

 – apply the brakes on both the vehicle and trailer

 – lower the landing gear

 – stow the handle away safely

 – turn off any taps fitted to the air lines

 – disconnect the air lines and stow them away safely

 – disconnect the electric lines and stow them away safely

 – remove any 'dog clip' securing the kingpin release handle

 – release the fifth wheel coupling locking bar, if fitted

 – drive the tractor unit away slowly, checking the trailer either directly or in the mirrors

 – take any anti-theft precautions (kingpin lock, etc.)

 – remove the number plate.

With a rigid vehicle and trailer you might have to support the trailer drawbar before you pull away.

The procedure for uncoupling a close-coupled articulated vehicle and trailer is given on page 216.

When recoupling you must

 – ensure the trailer brake is applied

 – check that the height of the trailer is correct so that it will receive the unit safely

 – reverse slowly up to the trailer ensuring that the kingpin locking mechanism is in place

 – ensure that the locking mechanism is secure by selecting a low gear and attempting to move forward

 – apply the parking brake before leaving the cab

 – connect any 'dog clip' to secure the kingpin release handle

- connect the air and electric lines

- turn on taps, if fitted

- raise the landing gear and stow away the handle

- ensure that the trailer brake is released before moving off

- check that all electrics are working

- start up the engine and ensure that the gauges register correct pressures in air storage tanks and that no warning buzzer/light is operating

- obtain assistance to check for air line leaks and operation of all rear, marker or reversing lights, indicators, stop lights and fog light(s)

- secure the correct number plate and check that all reflectors are present and clean

- examine all tyres, wheel nuts, fastenings, ropes, sheets, drop-side locking clips, rear doors, hydraulic rams, tail-lift gear, etc. to ensure that the trailer and any load won't present a danger to other road users

- check the function of any ABS warning lights, etc.

- make sure that your mirrors are properly adjusted to give the best view down each side of the trailer before driving off

- test the operation of the brakes at a safe place, ideally before moving out onto a public road.

When recoupling a rigid vehicle + trailer combination the sequence is similar, but the trailer drawbar will need to be adjusted to the correct height (often by means of a 'bottle' jack) before the towing vehicle reverses to recouple the trailer. Be on the alert for the safety of anyone at the rear of your vehicle who is assisting you to recouple the trailer.

The procedure for recoupling a close-coupled articulated vehicle is given on page 216.

Part Six

The LGV driving test

The topics covered

- Safety check questions
- The reversing exercise
- The braking exercise
- The vehicle controls
- Other controls
- The gear-changing exercise
- Moving off
- Using the mirrors
- Giving signals
- Acting on signs and signals
- Awareness and anticipation
- Making progress
- Controlling your speed
- Separation distance
- Hazards
- Selecting a safe place to stop
- Uncoupling and recoupling
- If you pass
- If you don't pass

Safety check questions

What the test requires

The examiner will ask you to demonstrate, or explain, how to carry out safety checks on your vehicle before driving. If you are taking a test in a rigid vehicle you will be asked to demonstrate, or explain, how to carry out five separate checks. The questions will be based on the skill list shown below.

Here are two examples of the type of question you might be asked.

- Show me how you would check the wheel nuts are secure on this vehicle.
- Tell me the main safety factors involved in loading this vehicle.

If you are taking a test in a vehicle towing a trailer, you will be asked to demonstrate or explain how to carry out two separate checks.

Skills you should show

You will be expected to know how to check that

- your tyres are correctly inflated, have a safe tread depth and are generally safe to use on the road
- your brakes are working effectively and the pedal does not have excessive travel
- your vehicle has sufficient oil, coolant and hydraulic fluid
- you have sufficient windscreen washer fluid
- the power assisted steering is working and that excessive free play is not apparent
- your headlights, tail lights and reflectors are working and clean
- your brake lights are working and clean
- your horn is working
- the wheel nuts and mud guards are secure

- the vehicle has sufficient air pressure
- all cargo doors are secure.

You will also be expected to know how to

- check for air leaks
- replace the tachometer disc
- check the windscreen wipers for wear and that the windscreen is clean
- check the suspension for defects
- load a vehicle safely
- ensure the load is secure.

For more information about vehicle safety checks see pages 41-57.

Faults to avoid

You should avoid

- being unfamiliar with the vehicle you are using on test
- being unable to explain or carry out safety checks on the vehicle you are using on test.

The reversing exercise

The exercise is started from a position with the front of the vehicle in line with cones A and A1. You should reverse your vehicle into the bay, keeping marker B on the offside. You should stop with the extreme rear of your vehicle within the stopping area.

From 1 September 2003, the stopping area will have both a solid yellow line and a yellow and black hatched section, and a barrier will be situated at the end of the reversing bay. You should stop with the extreme rear of your vehicle in the 75 cm wide yellow and black stopping area.

The distances

A to A1 = 1½ times the width of the vehicle

A to B = twice the length of the vehicle

B to line Z = 3 times the length of the vehicle*

The length of the bay will be based on the length of the vehicle. This can be varied at the discretion of the examiner within the range of 1 to 2 metres (3 to 6 feet).

*The maximum permitted length of a drawbar outfit on the road is now 18.75 metres (previously 18.35 metres). When setting out the area to accommodate a vehicle of this length the distance between cones A + A1 and cone B **must** be twice the length of the outfit. The bay should be set out as normal.

As indicated, the area is 92.5 metres in length and this can accommodate vehicles up to 18.5 metres long. For vehicles over 18.5 and up to 18.75 metres, cones A + A1 should be set on the yellow line and cone B should be positioned two vehicle lengths away. This will mean that for these larger vehicles the overall length of the area will be less than five times the length of the outfit.

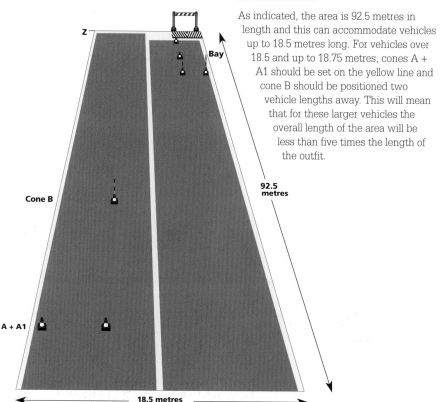

Z

Bay

92.5 metres

Cone B

A + A1

18.5 metres

What the test requires

You should be able to reverse your vehicle and trailer in a restricted space. You must be able to do this

- under control and in reasonable time
- with good observation
- with reasonable accuracy
- starting with the front of the vehicle at a fixed point (cones A and A1)
- inside a clearly defined boundary (yellow lines)
- by reversing so that you pass cone B on the offside of your vehicle
- so that the extreme rear of your vehicle or trailer is stopped within the 75 cm yellow and black stopping area and in a position to load or unload safely at the simulated loading platform.

Your examiner will show you a diagram of the manoeuvring area and explain what's required.

Skills you should show

You should complete the exercise

- reversing under complete control
- using good, effective, all-round observation
- ensuring accurate judgement of the size of your vehicle and trailer from the cab
- driving with careful co-ordination of the clutch, accelerator and footbrake until the exercise is completed.

Faults to avoid

You should avoid

- approaching the starting point too fast
- not driving in a straight line as you approach cones A and A1
- stopping beyond the first marker cones A and A1
- turning the steering wheel incorrectly when starting to reverse
- over-steering so that any wheel goes over the yellow boundary
- not practising effective observation or misjudging the position of your vehicle so that it comes in contact with any cone or pole
- incorrect judgement so that the rear of your vehicle and trailer is either short of or beyond the yellow and black stopping area in the bay
- using excessive steering movements or shunts to complete the manoeuvre
- when taking a forward shunt, driving down the area ahead of a position level with cones A and A1
- carrying out the manoeuvre at a very slow pace
- leaving the cab in order to satisfy yourself of the vehicle's position.

The braking exercise

There's no emergency stop exercise in the LGV driving test. For safety reasons a braking exercise takes place at a special area and not on the public roads.

What the test requires

Your examiner will be with you in the vehicle for this exercise.

She or he will point out two marker cones about 61 metres (200 feet) ahead. You should build up a speed of about 20 mph. When the front of the vehicle passes between the two markers you should apply the brakes.

You must stop your vehicle and trailer with safety and under full control.

Skills you should show

You should stop the vehicle

- as quickly as possible
- under full control
- as safely as possible
- in a straight line.

Faults to avoid

You should avoid

- driving too slowly (less than 20 mph)
- braking too soon (anticipating the marker points)
- braking too harshly, causing loss of control
- depressing the clutch well before the brake
- depressing the clutch too late, stalling the engine.

    (Note: For vehicles fitted with ABS, please refer to the vehicle handbook)

- taking too long to stop.

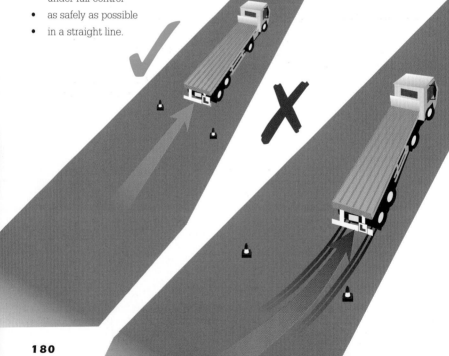

The vehicle controls

What the test requires

You must show your examiner that you understand the functions of all the controls. You should use them

- smoothly
- correctly
- safely
- at the right time.

The main controls are

- accelerator
- clutch
- footbrake
- handbrake
- steering
- gears.

You must

- understand what these controls do
- be able to use them competently.

How your examiner will test you

For this aspect of driving there isn't a special exercise. Your examiner will watch you carefully to see how you use these controls.

Skills you should show

Accelerator and clutch

You should

- balance the accelerator and clutch to pull away smoothly
- accelerate gradually to gain speed
- when stopping the vehicle, press the clutch in just before it stops.

If your vehicle has automatic transmission ensure that your foot is on the footbrake when you engage 'drive' (D).

Gears

The gears are designed to assist the engine to deliver power under a variety of conditions. The lowest gears may only be necessary if the vehicle is loaded or when climbing steep gradients. The gearbox may have one or more 'crawler' gear positions.

You should

- move off in the most suitable gear
- change gear in good time before a junction or hazard
- show an understanding of the type of gearbox you're using by demonstrating its abilities
- plan well ahead, whether climbing or before starting to descend a long hill.

If you leave it until you're either losing or gaining too much speed you may have difficulty selecting gears and maintaining control.

Modern vehicles may be fitted with sophisticated systems controlled by computer. These systems can sense the load, speed or gradient and select the correct gear for the conditions. With these systems the driver may only have to ease the accelerator, or depress the clutch pedal, to allow the system to engage the gear required.

If you're driving a vehicle with a 'range change' gearbox you should ensure that you've selected the correct range before changing gear.

Faults to avoid

Accelerator

You should avoid

- loud over-revving, causing excessive engine noise and exhaust fumes, and also alarming or distracting other road users.

Clutch

You should avoid

- jerky and uncontrolled use of the clutch when moving off or changing gear.

Gears

You should avoid

- taking your eyes off the road when you change gear
- 'coasting' with the clutch pedal depressed or leaving the gear lever in neutral. This is highly dangerous if you're driving a vehicle with air brakes. The engine-driven compressor won't be able to replace the air being used by the brakes due to the engine running only at idle speed

- holding onto the gear lever unnecessarily
- forgetting to move the range selector switch.

Skills you should show

Brake

You should brake

- in good time
- lightly, in most situations
- progressively.

Most large vehicles are equipped with air brake systems. There's no direct relationship between the pressure applied to the pedal and the braking force exerted on the wheels. This means that good control is needed at all times.

Faults to avoid

You should avoid

- braking harshly
- excessive and prolonged use of the footbrake
- braking and steering at the same time, unless already travelling at a low speed.

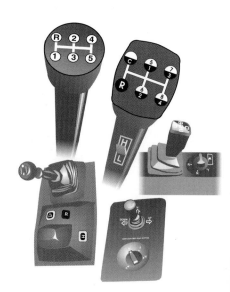

Skills you should show

Handbrake

You should know how and when to apply the handbrake effectively.

Some modern vehicles will apply a parking brake when the vehicle is brought to a stop by the footbrake.

Steering

You should

- place your hands on the steering wheel in a position that's comfortable and which gives you full control
- keep your movements steady and smooth
- turn the steering wheel to turn a corner at the correct time.

Power-assisted steering

Most modern vehicles are fitted with power assisted steering. The power assistance is often incorporated within the steering box or uses an engine-driven pump to supply hydraulic fluid under pressure, which operates 'rams' attached to the steering arms. Power assistance relieves the driver of steering effort, especially at slow speeds.

When the engine is running, hydraulic pressure is built up in the system to make the steering easier. If the steering becomes 'heavy', check for leaks in the system.

Do not attempt to turn the steering whilst stationary (known as 'dry steering'), as this will cause wear to the mechanism.

If a fault develops whilst travelling, stop as soon as you can safely do so and seek expert advice.

Faults to avoid

Handbrake

You should avoid

- applying the handbrake before the vehicle has stopped
- trying to move off with the handbrake on
- allowing the vehicle to roll back as you move off.

Steering

Don't steer too early when turning a corner. If you do, you risk

- cutting the corner when turning right, causing the rear wheels to cut across the path of traffic waiting to emerge
- striking the kerb when turning left.

Don't turn too late. You could put other road users at risk by

- swinging wide at left turns
- overshooting right turns.

Avoid

- crossing your hands on the steering wheel whenever possible
- allowing the wheel to spin back after turning
- resting your arm on the door.

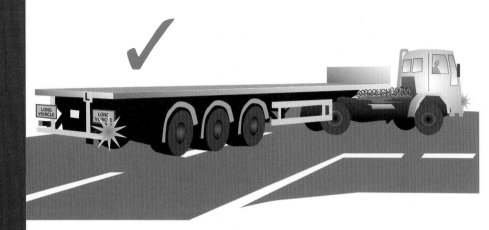

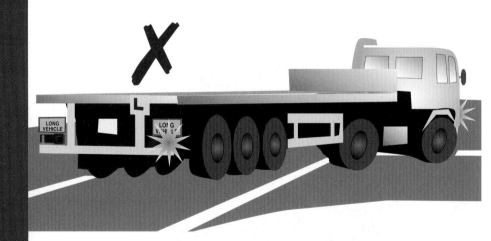

Other controls

You should understand

The functions of all controls and switches on your vehicle that have a bearing on road safety, such as

- indicators
- lights
- windscreen wipers
- demisters.

You should know the meaning of all gauges and switches on the instrument panel, such as

- air pressure gauges
- speedometer
- various warning lights and buzzers
- on-board computer displays
- ABS failure warnings
- bulb failure warnings
- gear-selection indicators.

Safety checks and fault recognition

You should be able to carry out routine checks, such as on

- steering
- brakes
- tyres
- seat belts
- lights
- reflectors
- horn
- rear view mirrors
- speedometer
- exhaust system
- direction indicators
- windscreen, wipers and washers
- wheel-nut security.

You should be able to understand the effect any fault may have on your vehicle.

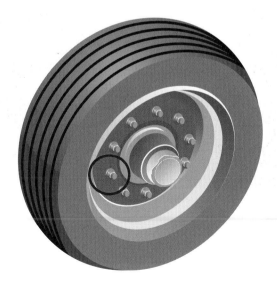

The gear-changing exercise

What the test requires

Your examiner wants to see you engage the lower gears competently. These gears may not otherwise be used during the drive.

You'll be asked to pull up at a convenient place to carry out the gear-changing exercise. Your examiner will then ask you to move off in your **lowest** gear and to change up to each gear in turn. If your vehicle has a 'crawler' gear, which requires the vehicle to be stationary when engaged, you won't be asked to use it during the gear-changing exercise.

Drive for a short distance in each gear until you reach a gear your examiner considers appropriate for your vehicle. This will depend on the gearbox layout.

When you've reached the highest gear your examiner will ask you to change back down into each gear in turn until you reach the lowest gear again.

Skills you should show

You should show

- a smooth start in the lowest gear
- good judgement of the correct speed for the next gear
- smooth engagement of the next lowest gear by bringing the speed of the vehicle down and by careful use of the footbrake, if necessary
- returning to the lowest gear without stopping the vehicle completely

Throughout the exercise you should

- practise effective observation, especially before moving off and slowing down
- give any signal that might be appropriate
- use the controls skilfully to ensure smooth engagement of the gears.

Faults to avoid

You should avoid

- not checking the blind spots before moving off or slowing down, and not acting on what you see in the mirrors
- jerky use of the clutch or accelerator
- not starting off in the lowest gear
- not selecting the next gear in the sequence
- not being able to engage a gear
- not giving a signal to any following traffic before slowing down.

Moving off

What the test requires

You should be able to move off safely and under control

- on the level
- from behind a parked vehicle
- uphill
- downhill.

How your examiner will test you

Your examiner will watch your use of the controls as you move off.

Skills you should show

Before you move off

- use your mirrors
- look all around your vehicle.

You should be aware of

- other vehicles
- cyclists
- pedestrians outside the range of your mirrors.

You should move off under control, making balanced and safe use of the

- accelerator
- clutch
- brakes
- steering
- correct gear.

Uphill

You should

- practise effective observation before moving off, checking all blind spots
- give a signal, if required, at the correct time
- use sufficient acceleration, depending on the gradient
- move off smoothly
- change up as soon as it's safe to do so.

Downhill

You should

- move off only when it's safe to do so
- practise effective observation before moving off, checking all blind spots
- give a signal, if required, at the correct time.

When you move off you should

- engage the correct gear for the gradient
- hold the vehicle on the footbrake and release the handbrake until it's safe to move away
- co-ordinate the clutch and accelerator
- build up speed when it's safe to do so.

Faults to avoid

Uphill

You should avoid moving off without

- using both nearside and offside mirrors
- looking around to check all blind spots
- giving a correct signal if it's required
- using enough revs for the gradient.

You should avoid moving off without good control of the accelerator, clutch and handbrake. Don't

- stall
- roll backwards
- surge away.

Downhill

You should avoid moving off without

- using both nearside and offside mirrors
- looking around to check all the blind spots
- giving a correct signal, if it's required
- co-ordinating the accelerator, clutch and handbrake so that the vehicle stalls or surges.

How your examiner will test you

At an angle

Your examiner will ask you to pull up on the left just before you reach a parked vehicle. You'll be asked to move away to show your ability to move off at an angle.

Skills you should show

When moving out from behind a parked vehicle you should

- practise effective all-round observation
- check any blind spots
- give a signal, if it's necessary
- move out only when it's safe to do so
- move out well clear of the parked vehicle
- check your mirrors, especially the nearside, to confirm that you're clear of the parked vehicle.

Faults to avoid

You should avoid

- pulling out unsafely
- causing other road users to stop or alter their course
- excessive acceleration
- moving off in too high a gear
- failing to co-ordinate the controls correctly and stalling the engine
- swinging excessively wide into the path of oncoming traffic.

Using the mirrors

What the test requires

You must always use your mirrors effectively

- before any manoeuvre
- to keep up to date on what's happening behind you.

Use them before

- moving off
- signalling
- changing direction
- turning left or right
- overtaking or changing lanes
- increasing speed
- slowing down or stopping
- opening your cab door.

Check again in your nearside mirror after passing

- parked vehicles
- horse riders, motorcyclists or cyclists
- any pedestrians standing close to the kerb
- any vehicle that you've just overtaken

before moving back into the left.

How your examiner will test you

For this aspect of driving there isn't a special exercise. Your examiner will watch you use your mirrors as you drive.

Skills you should show

Use the Mirrors – Signal – Manoeuvre (MSM) routine and also the Position – Speed – Look (PSL) routine. You should

- look before you signal
- signal before you act
- act sensibly on what you see in the mirrors
- be aware that the mirrors won't show everything behind you.

You should check your nearside mirror every time you pass

- parked vehicles
- vulnerable road users
- vehicles you've just overtaken
- pedestrians near the kerb.

Always have as good an idea of what's happening behind you as what's going on in front. You should also be aware of the effect your large vehicle has on other road users around you.

Giving signals

What the test requires

You must give clear signals in good time so that other road users know what you're about to do. This is particularly important with LGVs because other road users may not understand the position you need to move into

- before turning left
- before turning right
- at roundabouts
- to move off at an angle
- before reversing into an opening.

You should only give signals that are in *The Highway Code*.

Correct signals should help other road users to

- understand what you intend to do next
- take appropriate action.

Always check that you've cancelled an indicator as soon as it's safe to do so.

How your examiner will test you

For this aspect of driving there isn't a special exercise. Your examiner will watch you carefully to see how you use your signals as you drive.

Skills you should show

You should give signals

- clearly
- at the appropriate time
- by indicator
- by arm, if necessary.

Faults to avoid

You should avoid

- giving misleading or incorrect signals
- omitting to cancel signals
- waving on pedestrians to cross in front of your vehicle
- giving signals other than those shown in *The Highway Code*.

Acting on signs and signals

What the test requires

You should have a thorough knowledge of traffic signs, signals and road markings. You should be able to

- recognise them in good time
- take appropriate action on them.

At the start of the drive your examiner will ask you to follow the road ahead, unless traffic signs indicate otherwise or you're asked to turn. From this point your examiner will expect you to understand and act correctly on road signs or signals that occur.

Skills you should show

Traffic lights and signals

You should

- comply with traffic lights and signals
- approach at a speed that allows you to stop, if necessary, under full control
- only move forward at a green traffic light if it's clear for you to do so and you won't block the junction.

Authorised persons

You must comply with the signals given by

- police officers
- traffic wardens
- school crossing patrols

- Highways Agency Traffic Officers
- an authorised person controlling the traffic, e.g., at road repairs.
- Vehicle & Operator Services Agency Officers

Other road users

You should look out for signals given by other road users and

- react safely
- take appropriate action
- anticipate their action
- use your brakes and/or give arm signals, if necessary, to any traffic following your vehicle.

You need to be aware that, due to the size of your vehicle, road users behind you may not be able to see signals given by a vehicle ahead of you, for example if they are stopping or turning. Therefore, special care should be taken if you need to alter your speed or course as a result of a vehicle ahead of you carrying out such a manoeuvre.

Awareness and anticipation

What the test requires

You must be aware of other road users at all times. You should also always plan ahead and

- judge what other road users are going to do
- predict how their actions would affect you
- react safely and in good time.

Skills you should show

You should show

- awareness of and consideration for all other road users
- anticipation of possible danger and concern for safety.

Pedestrians

You should

- give way to pedestrians when turning from one road into another
- take particular care with the very young, the disabled and the elderly. They may not have seen you and might not be able to react quickly to danger.

Cyclists

Take special care

- when crossing bus or cycle lanes
- with cyclists passing on your left
- with child cyclists.

Moped riders and motorcyclists

Look out for mopeds and motorcyclists

- in slow-moving traffic
- coming up on your left
- at junctions.

Horse riders and animals

Take special care with people in charge of animals, especially horse riders.

Faults to avoid

You should avoid

- reacting suddenly to road or traffic conditions rather than anticipating them
- showing irritation with other road users
- sounding the horn aggressively
- revving your engine or edging forward when waiting for pedestrians to cross.

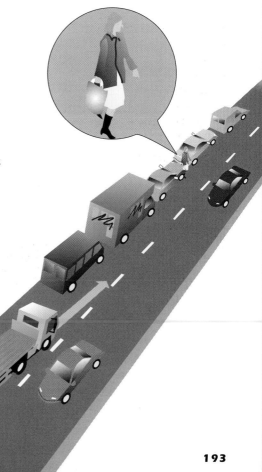

Making progress

Your examiner will be looking for a high standard of driving from an experienced driver. You'll need to display safe, confident, positive driving techniques.

How your examiner will test you

For this aspect of driving there isn't a special exercise. As an experienced driver you'll be expected to drive accordingly. Your examiner will watch your driving and expect you to make good progress safely.

Skills you should show

You should

- make reasonable progress where conditions allow
- keep up with the traffic flow when it's safe to do so
- make positive, safe decisions as you make progress.

You should be able to drive at the appropriate speed depending on the

- type of road
- weather conditions and visibility
- traffic conditions.

Approach all hazards at a safe speed without

- being unduly cautious
- holding up following traffic unnecessarily.

Faults to avoid

You should avoid

- driving so slowly that you hinder other traffic
- being over-cautious or hesitant
- stopping when you can see it's obviously clear and safe to go on.

Controlling your speed

What the test requires

You should make good progress along the road, taking into consideration

- the type of road
- the volume of traffic
- the weather conditions and the state of the road surface
- the braking characteristics of your vehicle
- speed limits that apply to your vehicle
- any hazards associated with the time of day (schools, etc.).

How your examiner will test you

For this aspect of driving there isn't a special exercise. Your examiner will watch you control your speed as you drive.

Skills you should show

You should

- take great care in the use of speed
- drive at the correct speed for the traffic conditions
- be sure that you can stop safely in the distance that you can see to be clear

- leave a separation distance between your vehicle and the traffic ahead
- allow extra stopping distance on a wet or slippery surface
- observe the speed limit that applies to your vehicle
- anticipate any hazards that could arise
- allow for the mistakes of others.

Faults to avoid

You should avoid

- driving too fast for the conditions
- exceeding speed limits
- varying your speed erratically
- having to brake hard to avoid a situation ahead
- approaching bends, traffic signals and any other hazards too fast.

Always keep a safe separation distance between you and the traffic in front.

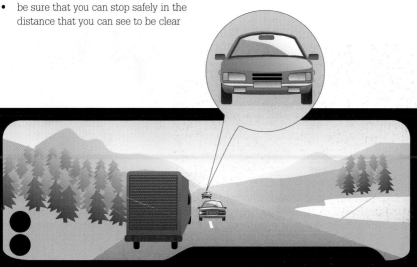

Separation distance

What the test requires

You should always drive so that you can stop safely in the distance you can see to be clear.

In good weather conditions, leave a gap of at least 1 metre (about 3 feet) for each mph of your speed, or a two-second time gap.

In bad conditions, leave at least double that distance, or a four-second time gap.

In slow-moving congested traffic it may not be practical to leave as much space.

How your examiner will test you

For this aspect of driving there isn't a special exercise. Your examiner will watch you as you drive and take account of your

- use of the MSM/PSL routine
- anticipation
- reaction to changing road and traffic conditions
- handling of the controls.

Skills you should show

You should

- judge a safe separation distance from the traffic in front
- show correct use of the MSM/PSL routine, especially before reducing speed

- avoid the need to brake sharply if the vehicle in front slows down or stops
- take extra care when your view ahead is limited by large vehicles
- keep a good separation distance from traffic queues in front.

Look out for

- brake lights ahead
- direction indicators
- vehicles ahead braking without warning.

Faults to avoid

You should avoid

- following too closely or 'tailgating'
- braking suddenly
- swerving to avoid the vehicle in front, which may be slowing down or stopping.

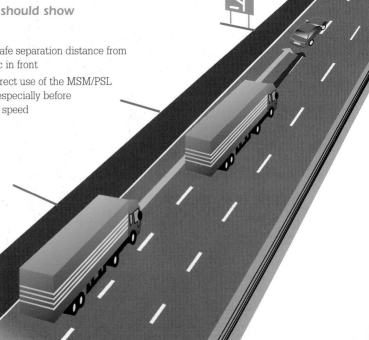

Hazards

What is a hazard?

A hazard may present itself when you're either stationary or on the move. Hazards may be included in any situation that involves you adjusting your speed or altering your course. In addition, hazards can be created by the actions of other road users around you. Look well ahead for

- road junctions or roundabouts
- parked vehicles
- cyclists or horse riders

- pedestrian crossings
- pedestrians on or near the kerbside
- cyclists or motorcyclists moving up alongside
- drivers edging up on the nearside before you make a turn
- vehicles pulling up close behind when you want to reverse.

Watch what's happening around you.

Traffic situations are constantly changing. These changes might depend on the

- time of day
- location
- density of traffic.

You should be aware and anticipate potential hazards when you drive.

Skills you should show

Your higher seat position in an LGV may mean that you're able to see more clearly some of the hazards around you. As a professional driver you must be able to anticipate what might happen. You should be driving with a sense of awareness and anticipation. Know

- what's happening ahead
- what other road users are about to do
- when to take action.

Scan the road ahead and be alert in case you have to

- speed up
- slow down
- prepare to stop
- change direction.

Hazards – other road users

Skills you should show

Pedestrians

Give way to pedestrians when turning from one road into another or when entering premises such as supermarkets, shops, warehouses, etc. Take extra care with the

- young
- elderly

and people who appear to have a disability.

Look out for pedestrians at all times but especially in shopping areas, where there might be a number of people waiting to cross the road, often at junctions.

Drive slowly and considerately when you need to enter pedestrianised areas to deliver to premises, during times when unloading or loading is permitted.

Cyclists

Take extra care when

- crossing cycle lanes
- you're about to turn left and you can see a cyclist near the rear of your vehicle or moving up along the nearside of your vehicle
- approaching any children on cycles
- there are gusty wind conditions.

Motorcyclists

Look out for motorcyclists who are

- 'filtering' in slow traffic streams
- moving up alongside your vehicle, especially the nearside.

Be especially aware when you're waiting to move out from a junction.

Think once

Think twice

Think bike.

Horse riders and animals

The size and noise of your vehicle can easily unsettle a horse. You should

- give riders as much room as is safe
- Slow down even if the horse and rider are on the grass verge rather than the road
- avoid revving the engine/releasing air brakes
- look out for young riders who are learning and might not be able to control their horses - (they may be on a leading rein with someone walking beside them)
- react in good time to anyone who is herding animals
- look out for warning signs, e.g., cattle.

Faults to avoid

You should avoid

- sounding the horn aggressively
- revving the engine and causing the air brakes to 'hiss'
- edging forward when pedestrians are crossing in front
- showing any sign of irritation.

Hazards – positioning and lane discipline

What the test requires

You should

- normally keep well to the left
- keep clear of parked vehicles
- avoid weaving in and out between parked vehicles
- position your vehicle correctly for the direction you intend to take.

You should obey all lane markings, especially

- left- or right-turn arrows at junctions
- when approaching roundabouts
- in one-way streets
- for bus lanes
- road markings for LGVs approaching arches or narrow bridges with restricted headroom.

How your examiner will test you

For this aspect of driving there isn't a special exercise. Your examiner will watch carefully to see that you

- use the MSM/PSL routine
- select the correct lane in good time.

Skills you should show

You should

- plan ahead and choose the correct lane in good time
- use the MSM/PSL routine correctly
- position your vehicle sensibly, even if there aren't any road markings
- be aware that other road users might not understand your actions, so signal in good time.

Faults to avoid

You should avoid

- driving too close to the kerb
- driving too close to the centre of the road
- changing lanes at the last moment or without good reason
- hindering other road users by being badly positioned or in the wrong lane
- straddling lanes or lane markings
- cutting across the path of other traffic in another lane at roundabouts.

There may be occasions, due to the length of your vehicle, when you have to straddle lane markings to avoid mounting the kerb or colliding with lamp-posts, traffic signs, etc. Use your own skill and judgement in making these decisions.

Hazards – junctions

What the test requires

The size of your vehicle means that it's essential to make the correct decisions at junctions. Look well ahead and assess the situation as you approach.

Judge carefully when it's safe to emerge. Act on what you see. Wait until you can see that it's clear, then move away safely.

If you don't know, don't go

Skills you should show

You should

- use the MSM/PSL routine in good time when you approach a junction or a roundabout
- assess the situation correctly so that you can position your vehicle to negotiate the junction safely
- take as much room as you need as you approach a junction, if you're driving a long rigid vehicle or a vehicle and trailer combination
- be aware of any lane markings and the fact that your vehicle may have to occupy part of the lane alongside
- position as early as it's practicable to do so in one-way streets
- make sure that you take **effective** observation before emerging into any junction.

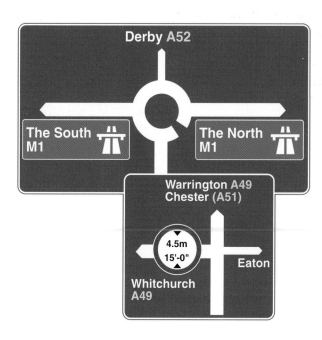

Left or right turns

Extra care should be taken if you're driving a long or an articulated vehicle, or a vehicle and trailer combination.

When turning left or right, position your vehicle so that you can

- see into the road
- turn without the rear/trailer wheels mounting the kerb
- turn without any part of the vehicle colliding with bollards or guard rails.

If you're crossing a dual carriageway or turning right onto one, don't move forward unless you can clear the centre reservation safely. If your vehicle is too long for the gap, wait until it's clear from both sides and there's a safe opportunity to go.

Always

- use your mirrors to check the rear wheels of your vehicle or trailer as you turn into or out of a junction
- assess the speed of oncoming traffic correctly before crossing or entering roads with fast-moving traffic
- allow for the fact that you'll need more time to build up speed in the new road.

Observe, assess, then judge before you act.

Hazards – roundabouts

What the test requires

Roundabouts can vary in size and complexity, but the object of them all is to allow traffic to flow wherever possible.

Some roundabouts are so complex or busy that they require traffic lights to control the volume of traffic. The lights may be used at peak times when the traffic becomes very heavy.

At the majority of roundabouts the approaching traffic is required to give way to traffic approaching from the right. There are some locations where a 'Give Way' sign and markings apply to traffic already on the roundabout. You must be aware of these differences.

Skills you should show

It's essential that you plan your approach well in advance and use the MSM/PSL routine in good time. It's most important that you get into the correct lane as you approach. You should know the exit you wish to take and choose the suitable lane, taking into consideration the size of your vehicle.

On approach

You should adjust the speed of your vehicle in good time on the approach to roundabouts. Check your speed and select the correct gear to negotiate the roundabout safely. Get into the correct lane. You should

- plan well ahead
- look out for traffic signs as you approach
- have a clear picture of the exit you intend to take
- look out for the number of exits before yours
- either follow the lane markings, as far as possible, or select the lane most suitable for the size of your vehicle
- use the MSM/PSL routine in good time
- signal your intentions in good time
- avoid driving into the roundabout too close to the right-hand kerb. If you're driving an articulated vehicle you'll have to steer to the left to avoid the roundabout kerb.

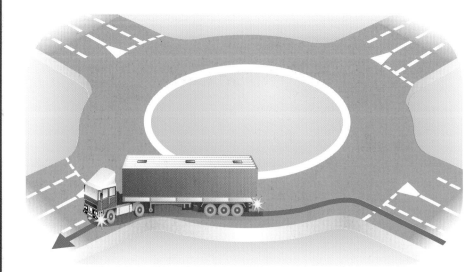

Whenever you enter a roundabout watch the vehicle in front of you. Make sure that it hasn't stopped while you were looking to the right. The driver ahead might be hesitant, so don't drive into the rear of it.

Turning left

You should

- give a left-turn signal in good time as you approach
- approach in the left-hand lane. If you're driving a long vehicle you might need to take some of the lane on your right

- adopt a path that ensures that the rear/trailer wheels don't mount the kerb
- give way to traffic approaching from the right
- use the nearside mirrors to be sure that no cyclists or motorcyclists are trapped along the nearside
- continue to signal through the turn
- look well ahead for traffic islands or bollards in the centre of your exit road. These could restrict the width available to you.

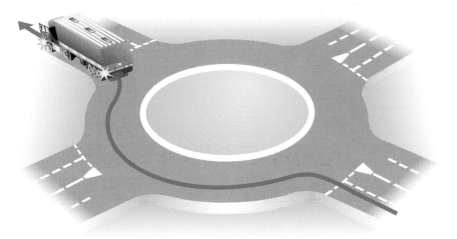

Going ahead

(Up to 12 o'clock on a clock face)

You should

- approach in the left-hand lane unless blocked or clearly marked for 'left turn' only
- don't give a signal on approach
- try to stay in the lane, depending on the length of your vehicle
- keep checking the mirrors both nearside and offside

- give way to traffic from the right, if necessary
- indicate left as you pass the exit just before the one that you intend to take
- look well ahead for traffic islands or bollards in the centre of your exit road
- make sure that the rear/trailer wheels don't mount the kerb as you leave the roundabout.

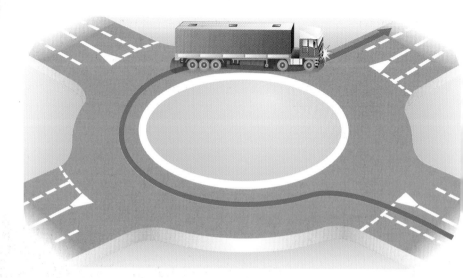

Turning right or full circle

You should

- look well ahead and use the MSM/PSL routine

- with a long vehicle, if there's a choice of two lanes for turning right use the left-hand of the two lanes. If only one lane is marked for right turns you might have to occupy part of the lane on your left, not only on approach, but also through the roundabout

- signal right in good time before moving over to the right on approach

- look out for any traffic accelerating up on the offside of your vehicle.

Mini-roundabouts

You might have restricted room, so keep a constant check in the mirrors. You should

- give way to the traffic from the right
- position your vehicle correctly on approach so that you don't mount any kerbs
- understand that other road users might not be aware of the room you need to complete a turn.

Multiple roundabouts

Plan your approach early. You should

- ensure that your eventual exit is clear so that you don't block the roundabout
- give clear signals
- look out for road users carrying out U-turns.

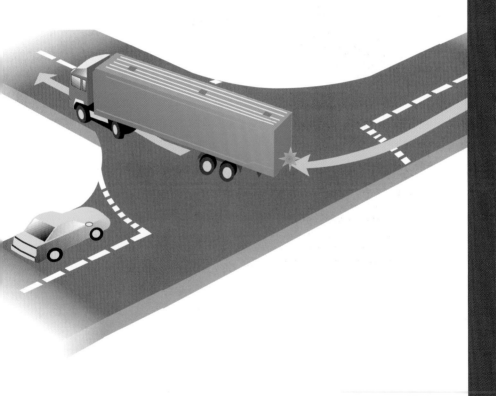

In a number of locations complex roundabout systems have been designed, which incorporate a mini-roundabout at each exit. The main thing to remember at such places is that traffic will be travelling in all directions. You must give way to traffic on the right.

Road surfaces

At the entrances to roundabouts there will have been a great deal of braking and accelerating. This will often make the road surface slippery, especially when it's wet.

You should

- brake in good time
- enter the roundabout ensuring that other road users don't have to brake suddenly or swerve.

Cyclists and horse riders

These road users might be in the left-hand lane on approach, but may intend to turn right. Be aware of this, and give them plenty of room.

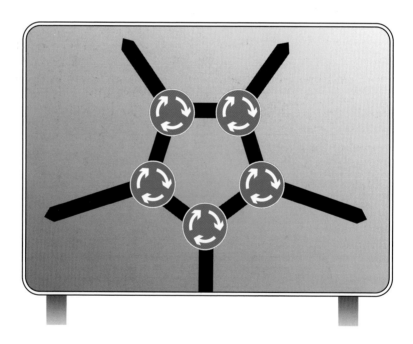

Hazards – overtaking

What the test requires

Before overtaking you should look well ahead for any hazards, such as

- oncoming traffic
- bends
- junctions
- the vehicle in front about to overtake
- any gradient
- those pointed out by road markings or traffic signs.

You should assess the

- speed of the vehicle that you intend to overtake
- speed differential of the two vehicles, to judge how long the manoeuvre could take
- time you have to complete overtaking safely.

Avoid the need to 'cut in' on the vehicle that you've just overtaken.

How your examiner will test you

For this aspect of driving there isn't a special exercise. Your examiner will watch you and take account of your

- use of the MSM/PSL routine
- reaction to road and traffic conditions
- handling of the controls
- choice of a safe opportunity to overtake.

Skills you should show

You should be able to assess all the factors that will decide if you can or can't overtake safely, such as

- oncoming traffic
- the type of road
- the speed of the vehicle ahead
- continuous white line markings on your side of the road
- how far ahead the road is clear
- whether the road will remain clear
- whether traffic behind is about to overtake your vehicle.

Only overtake where you can do so safely, legally and without causing other road users to slow down or alter course.

Faults to avoid

Don't overtake when

- your view of the road ahead isn't clear
- you would have to exceed the speed limit
- to do so would cause other road users to slow down or stop
- there are signs or road markings that prohibit overtaking.

Hazards – meeting and passing other vehicles

What the test requires

You should be able to meet and deal with oncoming traffic safely and confidently

- on narrow roads
- where there are obstructions such as parked cars
- where you have to move into the path of oncoming traffic.

How your examiner will test you

For this aspect of driving there isn't a special exercise. Your examiner will watch you and take account of your

- use of the MSM/PSL routine
- reactions to road and traffic conditions
- handling of the controls.

Skills you should show

You should

- show good judgement when meeting other traffic
- be decisive when stopping and moving off
- stop in a position that allows you to move out smoothly when the way is clear
- allow adequate clearance when passing stationary vehicles. Slow right down if you have to pass close to them.

Look out for

- doors opening
- children running out
- pedestrians stepping out from between parked cars or from buses
- vehicles pulling out without warning.

Faults to avoid

Avoid causing other vehicles to

- slow down
- swerve
- stop.

Avoid

- passing too close to parked vehicles
- using the size of your vehicle to force other traffic to give way.

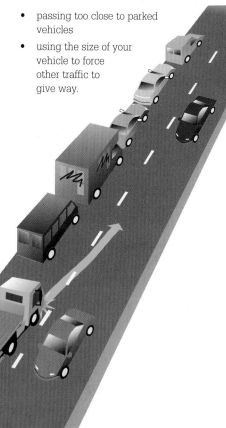

Hazards – crossing the path of other vehicles

What the test requires

You should be able to cross the path of oncoming traffic safely and with confidence. You'll need to do this when you

- turn right at a road junction
- enter premises on the right-hand side of the road.

You should

- use the MSM/PSL routine
- position the vehicle as correctly as possible, depending on the size of your vehicle
- assess accurately the speed of any approaching traffic
- wait if necessary
- look into the road entrance into which you're about to turn
- look out for any pedestrians.

How your examiner will test you

For this aspect of driving there isn't a special exercise. Your examiner will watch you and take account of your judgement of oncoming traffic.

Skills you should show

You should

- make safe and confident decisions about when to turn across the path of vehicles approaching from the opposite direction
- ensure that the road or entrance is clear for you to enter

- be confident that your vehicle won't endanger any road user waiting to emerge from the right
- assess whether it's safe to enter the road entrance
- show courtesy and consideration to other road users, especially pedestrians.

Faults to avoid

You should avoid

- cutting the corner
- overshooting the turn so that the front wheels mount the kerb
- turning across the path of any oncoming traffic, causing them to
  - slow down
  - swerve
  - stop.

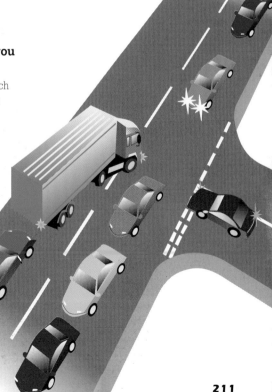

Hazards – pedestrian crossings

What the test requires

You should

- recognise the different types of pedestrian crossing
- show courtesy and consideration towards pedestrians
- stop safely when necessary.

How your examiner will test you

For this aspect of the test there isn't a special exercise. Your examiner will watch you carefully to see that you

- recognise the pedestrian crossing in good time
- use the MSM/PSL routine
- stop when necessary.

Skills you should show

Controlled crossings

These crossings may be controlled by traffic signals at junctions or by

- police officers
- traffic wardens
- school crossing patrols.

Slow down in good time and stop if you're asked to do so.

Zebra crossings

These crossings are recognised by

- black and white stripes across the road
- flashing amber beacons on both sides of the road
- tactile paving on both sides of the crossing
- zigzag road markings on both sides of the crossing.

You should

- slow down and stop if there's anyone on the crossing
- slow down and be prepared to stop if there's anyone waiting to cross.

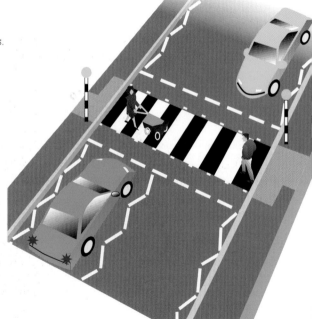

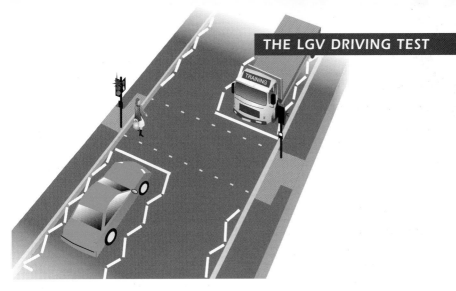

Pelican crossings

These crossings have traffic signals that are activated by pedestrians pressing a button on the panel at either side of the crossing. There's a flashing amber phase that allows pedestrians who are already on the crossing to continue to cross safely.

There are also zigzag lines on each side of the crossing and a stop line at the crossing.

You must

- stop if the lights are red or steady amber
- give way to any pedestrians crossing if the amber lights are flashing
- approach all crossings at a controlled speed
- stop safely when necessary
- only move off when it's safe to do so
- be especially alert
  - near schools
  - at shopping areas
  - when turning at junctions.

Puffin crossings

This type of crossing has been installed at a number of selected sights. They have infra-red detectors sited so that the red traffic signal phase may be held until pedestrians have cleared the crossing. No flashing amber is then necessary. The traffic signals operate in the normal sequence.

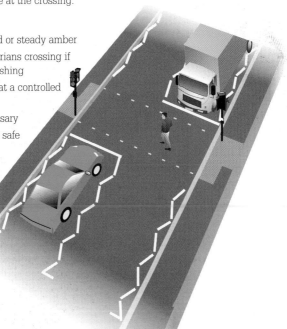

Toucan crossings

There are a few of these crossings installed throughout the country. They're usually found where there are large numbers of cyclists.

The cyclists share the crossing with pedestrians without having to dismount. They're shown a green cycle light when it's safe to cross.

Pegasus crossings

These are especially for horses and riders and have higher controls, a wooden fence along the kerb and a wider crossing area. Be especially aware of the danger that excess or sudden vehicle noise, air brake release or flashing lights could cause.

Faults to avoid

You should avoid

- approaching any type of crossing at too high a speed
- driving on without stopping or showing awareness of pedestrians waiting to cross
- driving onto or blocking a crossing
- overtaking within the zigzag lines
- waving pedestrians to cross
- revving the engine
- causing unnecessary air brake noise
- sounding the horn.

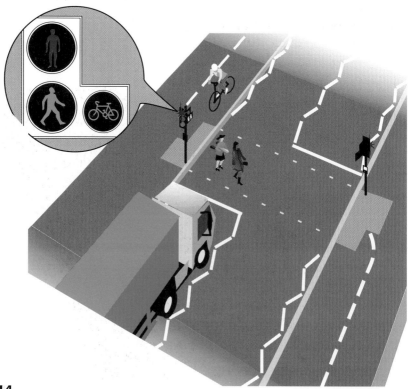

Selecting a safe place to stop

What the test requires

When you make a normal stop you must be able to select a safe place where you won't

- cause an obstruction
- create a hazard
- be illegally parked.

You should stop reasonably close to the kerb.

How your examiner will test you

At some stage during the test your examiner will ask you to pull up on the left at a convenient place.

Skills you should show

When selecting a safe place to stop

- identify it in good time
- make proper use of the MSM/PSL routine
- only stop where you're allowed to do so
- don't cause an obstruction
- recognise in good time road markings or signs indicating any restriction

- pull up close to and parallel with the kerb
- apply the parking brake while the vehicle is stationary
- stop at the correct place when asked.

Faults to avoid

You should avoid

- pulling up with late warning to other road users
- causing danger or inconvenience to other road users
- stopping at or outside
  - school entrances
  - fire or ambulance stations
  - bus stops
  - pedestrian crossings

You must comply with

- 'No Waiting' signs or markings
- 'No Parking' signs or markings
- other 'no stopping' restrictions.

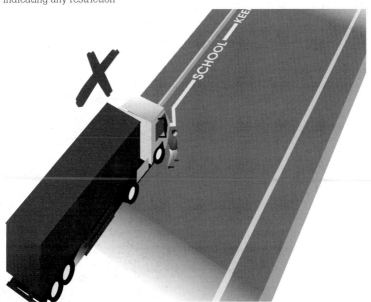

Uncoupling and recoupling

What the test requires

You should know and be able to demonstrate how to uncouple and recouple your vehicle and trailer safely.

Uncoupling

When uncoupling you should

- ensure that the brakes are applied on both the vehicle and trailer
- lower the landing gear and stow the handle away safely
- turn off any taps fitted to the air lines
- disconnect the air lines (sometimes referred to as 'suzies') and stow the lines away safely
- disconnect the electric line and stow it away safely
- remove any 'dog clip' securing the kingpin release handle
- release the fifth wheel coupling locking bar, if fitted
- drive the tractive unit away slowly, checking the trailer either directly or in the mirrors.

If you're driving a rigid vehicle with a trailer, you might have to support the trailer drawbar before you pull away. The 'suzies' on a draw-bar trailer are left with the trailer and should be left in a safe position, for example laid over the draw-bar.

For drivers of articulated vehicles with close-coupled trailers, the uncoupling sequence is as follows

- ensure that the brakes are applied on both the tractive unit and the trailer
- lower the landing gear and stow the handle away safely
- disconnect the 'dog clip' (if fitted) and release the fifth wheel coupling

- drive the tractive unit far enough forward so that you can stand on the catwalk
- turn off any taps fitted to the air lines
- disconnect the air lines (or 'suzies') and electrical connections and stow safely
- drive the tractive unit away slowly, checking the trailer either directly or in the mirrors.

Recoupling

When recoupling

- ensure that the trailer brake is applied
- check that the height of the trailer is correct so that it will receive the unit safely
- reverse slowly up to the trailer until you hear the kingpin mechanism locking into place
- select a low gear and try to move forward in order to test that the locking mechanism is secure. Do this twice to make sure
- ensure that the vehicle parking brake is applied
- connect any 'dog clip' to secure the kingpin release handle
- connect the air and electric lines. Turn on taps, if fitted
- raise the landing gear and stow away the handle
- release the trailer parking brake
- start up the engine
- check that the air is building up in the storage tanks
- check the trailer lights and indicators.

For drivers of articulated vehicles with close-coupled trailers, the recoupling sequence is as follows

- ensure that the trailer brake is applied

- reverse slowly up to the trailer, stop just short and apply the tractive unit parking brake

- check that the height of the trailer is correct so that it will receive the unit safely

- reverse back far enough under the trailer so that you can stand on the catwalk

- apply the tractive unit parking brake

- connect the air and electric lines. Turn on taps, if fitted

- reverse under the trailer and connect the fifth wheel

- select a low gear and try to move forward in order to test that the locking mechanism is secure. Do this twice to make sure

- apply the tractive unit parking brake

- connect any 'dog clip' to secure the kingpin release handle

- raise the landing gear and stow away the handle

- release the trailer parking brake

- start up the engine

- check that air is building up in the storage tanks

- check all the lights and indicators.

How your examiner will test you

You'll normally be asked to uncouple and recouple your vehicle and trailer at the end of the test. Your examiner will ask you to do this where there's safe and level ground.

You'll be asked to

- demonstrate the uncoupling of your vehicle and trailer

- pull forward and park the vehicle alongside the trailer

- realign the vehicle with the trailer before recoupling the trailer

- recouple the vehicle and trailer.

Your examiner will expect you to make sure that the

- coupling is secure

- lights and indicators are working

- trailer brake is released.

Skills you should show

You should be able to uncouple and recouple your vehicle and trailer

- safely
- confidently and in good time
- showing concern for your own and others' health and safety.

Faults to avoid

When uncoupling

You should avoid

- uncoupling without applying the brakes on the towing vehicle
- releasing the trailer coupling without the legs being lowered
- moving forward before the entire correct procedure has been completed.

When recoupling

You should avoid

- not checking the brakes are applied on the trailer
- not using good, effective observation around your trailer as you reverse up to it
- recoupling at speed
- leaving the cab without applying the vehicle's parking brake

Don't attempt to move away without checking the

- lights
- indicators
- trailer brake function.

Note

During the practical test you won't be asked to move your vehicle away after recoupling. You should, however, be aware of the safety precautions for this given in the official syllabus (see pages 172-173).

If you pass

Well done. You've demonstrated that you can drive an unladen LGV to the high standard required to obtain a vocational licence.

You'll be given

- a pass certificate (D10V)
- a copy of the driving test report (DLV25), which will show any driving faults that have been marked during the test.

You'll also be offered a brief explanation of any driving faults marked. This is to help you to overcome any weaknesses in your driving as you gain experience.

To apply for your full licence

- complete a D750 form to apply for a photocard licence
- enclose your licence
- enclose the pass certificate (D10V) with the applicant's declarations section signed
- enclose the appropriate fee.

Send to

The Vocational Section
DVLA
Swansea
SA99 1BR

as soon as you can (or in any case within two years).

After you've passed

You should always aim to improve your driving standards. Experience will present situations that you may not have encountered before. Learn from these and this will increase your ability to become a safe and reliable professional driver. Speak to your trainer about learning to drive laden vehicles.

If you don't pass

Your driving hasn't reached the high standard required to obtain the vocational licence. You've made mistakes that either caused or could have caused danger on the road.

Your examiner will give you

- a statement of failure including the driving test report (DLV25A), which will show all the faults marked during the test

- an explanation of why you failed.

You should study the driving test report carefully and refer to the relevant sections in this book.

Show the report to your instructor, who will help you to correct the points of failure. Listen to the advice your instructor gives and try to get as much practice as you can before you retake your test.

Right of appeal

Although your examiner's decision can't be altered, you have the right to appeal if you consider that your driving test wasn't conducted according to the regulations.

If you live in England or Wales you have six months after the issue of the statement of failure in which to appeal (Magistrates' Courts Act 1952, Ch. 55 part VII, Section 104). If you live in Scotland you have 21 days in which to appeal (Sheriff Court, Scotland Act of Sederunt (Statutory Appeals) 1981).

See also the DSA complaints guide for test candidates on page 223.

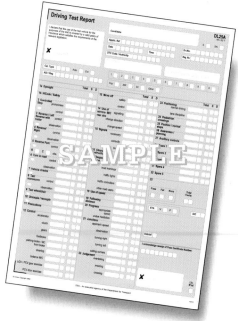

Part Seven

Additional information

The topics covered

- Disqualified drivers
- DSA services
- DSA offices
- LGV test centres
- Traffic Commissioners and Traffic Area offices
- Other useful addresses
- Categories of LGV licences
- Minimum test vehicles (MTVs)
- New MTV requirements
- Cone positions
- Glossary
- Hazard labels

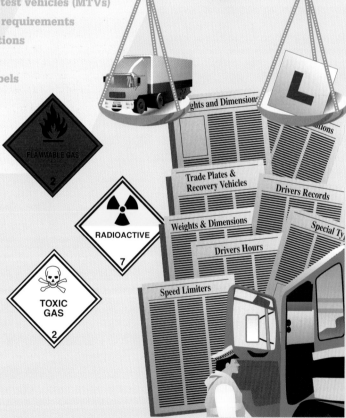

Disqualified drivers

Retesting once disqualified

Tougher penalties now exist for anyone convicted of certain dangerous driving offences. If a driver is convicted of a dangerous driving offence they'll lose all LGV entitlement.

The decision as to whether they'll be required to undergo an extended car driving test before they're allowed to drive an LGV again rests with the courts.

An LGV driving licence can't stand on its own. You must also possess a valid full driving licence for category B (that is, a car licence). If you lose your category B licence entitlement you also lose your LGV licence.

Applying for a retest

A person subject to a category B retest can apply for a provisional licence at the end of the period of disqualification.

The normal rules for provisional licence-holders apply

- the driver must be supervised by a person who's at least 21 years old and has held (and still holds) a full licence for at least three years for the category of vehicle being driven
- L plates (or D plates, if you wish, in Wales) must be displayed to the front and rear of the vehicle
- driving on motorways isn't allowed
- LGVs may not be driven on a provisional car licence (category B).

Having passed a category B extended test, an LGV driver has to apply to the Traffic Commissioner for their LGV licence. The return of the licence is at the discretion of the Traffic Commissioner, who can order a retest if he considers that it is necessary.

A further retest is not ordered in all cases.

DSA Service Standards

The Driving Standards Agency (DSA) is committed to providing a high-quality service for all its customers. If you would like information about our standards of service please contact

Customer Service Unit
Driving Standards Agency
Stanley House
Talbot Street
Nottingham NG1 5GU

Tel: 0115 901 2500/2545
Fax: 0115 901 2510
Email: customer.services@dsa.gsi.gov.uk

Refund of out-of-pocket expenses

DSA will normally refund the fee, or rebook your test at no further charge, where

- an appointment is cancelled by DSA – for any reason

- an appointment is cancelled by the candidate, who gives at least ten clear working days' notice

- the candidate keeps the test appointment, but the test doesn't take place or isn't completed for reasons not attributable to him or her nor to any vehicle provided for the test by the candidate.

In addition, DSA will normally consider reasonable claims from the candidate for financial loss or expenditure unavoidably and directly incurred by him or her as a result of DSA cancelling the test at short notice (other than for reasons of bad weather). For example, a claim for the commercial hire of the vehicle for the test will normally be considered. Applications should be made to the Area Office where the test was booked.

This compensation code doesn't affect your existing legal rights.

Complaints guide

DSA aims to give its customers the best possible service. Please tell us

- when we've done well
- when you aren't satisfied.

Your comments can help us to improve the service we have to offer.

If you have any questions about how your test was conducted please contact the local Supervising Examiner, whose address is displayed at your local driving test centre. If you're dissatisfied with the reply or you wish to comment on other matters you can write to the Regional Manager. (See the list of Area Offices at the back of this book.).

If your concern relates to an Approved Driving Instructor you should write to

The Registrar of Approved
Driving Instructors
Driving Standards Agency
Stanley House
Talbot Street
Nottingham NG1 5GU

Finally, you can write to

The Chief Executive
Driving Standards Agency
Stanley House
Talbot Street
Nottingham
NG1 5GU

If you remain dissatisfied, you can ask the Chief Executive to refer your complaint to the Independent Complaints Assessor. None of this removes your right to take your complaint to

- your Member of Parliament, who may decide to raise your case personally with the DSA Chief Executive, the Minister, or the Parliamentary Commissioner for Administration (the Ombudsman)

  Ann Abraham
  Millbank Tower
  Millbank
  London SW1P 4QP

  Tel: 0845 015 4033

- a magistrates' court (in Scotland to the Sheriff of your area) if you believe that your test wasn't carried out according to the regulations.

Before doing this you should seek legal advice.

DSA offices

Head Office

Stanley House
56 Talbot Street
Nottingham NG1 5GU

Tel: 0115 901 2500

National Telephone Numbers

For telephone bookings by Credit or Debit
Card and other enquiries: 0870 01 01 372
Fax applications: 0870 01 02 372
Welsh speakers: 0870 01 00 372
Minicom users: 0870 01 07 372

Postal applications

All postal applications should be sent to

DSA
PO Box 280
Newcastle-upon-Tyne
NE99 1FP

LGV test centres

You'll find LGV driving test centres in the
following places. Some test centres aren't
open full-time. Contact the national
telephone numbers for details of the full
office address and telephone number.

Scotland

Aberdeen

Benbecula*

Bishopbriggs (Glasgow)

Dumfries

Elgin

Galashiels

Inverness

Kilmarnock

Kirkwall

Lerwick

Livingstone (Edinburgh)

Machrihanish (Kintyre)*

Perth

Port Ellen*

Portree*

Stornoway

Wick

*Tests are only conducted occasionally at
these centres.

Northern

Berwick-on-Tweed

Beverley

Bredbury (Manchester)

Carlisle

Darlington

Gosforth (Newcastle)

Grimsby

Kirkham (Preston)

Patrick Green (Leeds)

Sheffield

Simonswood

Steeton (Keighley)

Walton (York)

Wales and Western

Bristol

Caernarfon

Camborne

Chiseldon (Swindon)

Exeter

Gloucester

Haverfordwest (Withybush)

Llantrisant

Neath

Plymouth

Pontypool

Poole

Reading

Rookley (Isle of Wight)

Southampton

Taunton

Wrexham

Midlands and Eastern

Alvaston (Derby)

Chelmsford

Culham

Featherstone (Wolverhampton)

Garretts Green (Birmingham)

Harlescott (Shrewsbury)

Ipswich

Leicester

Leighton Buzzard

Norwich

Peterborough

Swynnerton (Stoke-on-Trent)

Watnall (Nottingham)

Weedon (Northampton)

London and the South-East

Canterbury

Croydon

Enfield

Gillingham

Guildford

Hastings

Lancing

Purfleet

Yeading

Traffic Commissioners and Traffic Area Offices

Scotland

J Floor
Argyll House
3 Lady Lawson Street
Edinburgh EH3 9SE

Tel: 0131 200 4955
Fax: 0131 529 8501

Area covered:

All Scotland and the Islands.

North-Eastern and North-Western Traffic Area

Hillcrest House
386 Harehills Lane
Leeds LS9 6NF

Tel: 0113 254 3290/1

Fax: 0113 248 9607

Area covered:

Blackburn with Darwen

Blackpool

Cheshire

Cumbria

Darlington

Derby City

Derbyshire

Durham

East Riding of Yorkshire

Greater Manchester

Halton

Hartlepool

Kingston upon Hull

Lancashire

Merseyside

Middlesbrough

North Lincolnshire

North-East Lincolnshire

North Yorkshire

Northumberland

Nottingham

Nottinghamshire

Redcar & Cleveland

South Yorkshire

Stockton-on-Tees

Tyne & Wear

Warrington

West Yorkshire

York

Wales and West Midlands

Cumberland House
200 Broad Street
Birmingham B15 1TD

Wales

Tel: 0121 609 6835

West Midlands

Tel: 0121 609 6813

Fax for both areas

0121 608 1001

Area covered: West Midlands

Herefordshire

Shropshire

Staffordshire

Stoke-on-Trent

Telford

Warwickshire

West Midlands

Worcestershire

Wrekin

Area covered: Wales

All of Wales

Eastern

Terrington House
13–15 Hills Road
Cambridge CB2 1NP

Tel: 01223 531 060
Fax: 01223 532 089

Area covered:

Bedfordshire
Buckinghamshire
Cambridgeshire
Essex
Hertfordshire
Leicester
Leicestershire
Lincolnshire
Luton
Milton Keynes
Norfolk
Northamptonshire
Peterborough
Rutland
Southend-on-Sea
Suffolk
Thurrock

Western

2 Rivergate
Temple Quay
Bristol BS1 6EH

Tel: 0117 900 8577

Area covered:

Bath & North-East Somerset
Bournemouth
Bracknell Forest
Bristol
Cornwall
Devon
Dorset
Gloucestershire

Hampshire
Isle of Wight
North Somerset
Oxfordshire
Plymouth
Poole
Portsmouth
Reading
Slough
Somerset
Southampton
South Gloucestershire
Swindon
Torbay
West Berkshire
Wiltshire
Windsor & Maidenhead
Wokingham

South-Eastern and Metropolitan London

Ivy House
3 Ivy Terrace
Eastbourne BN21 4QT

Tel: 01323 452 400
Fax: 01323 726 679

Area covered:

Brighton and Hove
East Sussex
Greater London
Kent
Medway Towns
Surrey
West Sussex

Other useful addresses

The Association of Lorry Loader Manufacturers and Importers of Great Britain (ALLMI)

14 Manor Close
Droitwich
Worcestershire
WR9 8HG

Tel: 07071 226 773
Fax: 01905 770 892

City and Guilds London Institute

1 Giltspur Street
London
EC1 9DD

Tel: 020 7294 2468

Department for Transport (DfT) Mobility Advice and Vehicle Information Service (MAVIS)

'O' Wing, MacAdam Avenue
Old Wokingham Road
Crowthorne
RG45 6XD

Tel: 01344 661000
Fax: 01344 661066

Driver and Vehicle Licensing Agency (DVLA) DVLA Customer Enquiry Unit – Licence Enquiries

Swansea
SA6 7JL

Tel: 0870 240 0009
Minicom: 01792 782 787
Fax: 01792 783 071

(Service available Monday to Friday between 8.15 am and 8.30 pm, and Saturdays between 8.30 am and 5.00 pm)

DVLA Drivers' Medical Group

Swansea
SA99 1TU

Tel: 0870 600 0301

Freight Transport Association Ltd

Hermes House
St John's Road
Tunbridge Wells
Kent
TN4 9UZ

Tel: 01892 526171
Website: www.fta.co.uk

Historic Commercial Vehicle Society

Iden Grange
Cranbrook Road
Staplehurst
Kent
TN12 0ET

Tel: 01580 892 929
Fax: 01580 893 227
Email: hcvs@btinternet.com
Website: www.hcvs.co.uk

HSE Infoline

HSE Information Services
Caerphilly Business Park
Caerphilly
CF83 3GG

Tel: 0870 154 5500
Fax: 02920 859 260

(See your telephone book for details of your local HSE office.)

The Institute of Logistics and Transport

Logistics and Transport Centre
PO Box 5787
Corby
Northamptonshire
NN17 4XQ

Tel: 01536 740 100
Fax: 01536 740 101
Email: enquiry:iolt.org.uk
Website: www.iolt.org.uk

Road Haulage Association Ltd (RHA)

Roadway House
35 Monument Hill
Weybridge
Surrey
KT13 8RN

Tel: 01932 841 515
Fax: 01932 852 516

The Road Operator's Safety Council

395 Cowley Road
Oxford
OX4 2DJ

Tel: 01865 775 552
Fax: 01865 711 745

Royal Society for the Prevention of Accidents (RoSPA)

Edgbaston Park
353 Bristol Road
Birmingham
B5 7ST

Tel: 0121 248 2000
Fax: 0121 248 2001

RTITB

Ercall House
8 Pearson Road
Central Park
Telford
TF2 9TX

Tel: 01952 520200
Fax: 01952 520201

Vehicle and Operator Services Agency (VOSA)

(formerly Transport Area Network and the Vehicle Inspectorate)

The Enquiry Unit
Welcombe House
91-92 The Strand
Swansea
SA1 2DA

Tel: 0870 606 0440
Fax: 01792 454 313

Categories of LGV licences

Category	Description
C1	Medium-sized goods vehicle 3.5–7.5 tonnes, with a trailer up to 750kg
C1 + E	Medium-sized goods vehicle 3.5–7.5 tonnes plus a trailer above 750kg
C	Large goods vehicle above 3.5 tonnes, with a trailer up to 750kg
C + E	Large goods vehicle above 3.5 tonnes with a trailer above 750kg

Motorhomes and recreational vehicles come under either category C or C1, depending on their MAM. If used on test, they must meet the MTV requirements for the relevant category.

Minimum test vehicles (MTVs)

Category	Description
C1	Vehicle of at least 4 tonnes and capable of 80 km/h (50 mph)
C1 + E	Category C1 test vehicle with trailer of at least 2 tonnes, a combined length of at least 8 metres*, and capable of 80 km/h (50 mph)
C	Vehicle of at least 10 tonnes, at least 7 metres in length and capable of at least 80 km/h (50 mph)
C + E	An articulated vehicle of at least 18 tonnes and 12 metres in length, capable of 80 km/h (50mph); or a combination of a category C test vehicle with a trailer of at least 4 tonnes and a platform of at least 4 metres in length and with a combined weight of at least 18 tonnes and a combined length of 12 metres. The trailer is to operate with the appropriate service brakes and a heavy duty coupling arrangement suitable for the weight.

* This could be towing a trailer or articulated.

All the above weights refer to the maximum authorised mass (MAM).

Vehicles and trailers used for tests must be unladen. Small, properly secured items and fitted equipment are not considered to be a load.

If a skeleton trailer is used on test, it should be fitted with a container. Containers and demountable bodies are not considered a burden for driving test purposes.

A vehicle displaying trade plates is not suitable for a driving test, as the conditions attached to trade licences do not allow for a vehicle to be used for this purpose.

New regulations

In September 2000, the European Commission amended the minimum driving test requirements that must be adopted by all member states so that testing arrangements are kept relevant to modern driving and riding conditions.

Changes to driving test arrangements include more demanding minimum test vehicle requirements, including larger and heavier vehicles for lorry, bus and vehicle-trailer tests. The additional requirements are shown in the table below.

New MTV requirements for vehicles used for driving tests will apply to all vehicles brought into first use (first registration) from 1 October 2003. Vehicles brought into first use (first registration) before 1 October 2003 that meet the previoust MTV standards can be used for driving tests until the end of June 2007.

Further information and advice can be obtained on DSA's website: www.driving-tests.co.uk, or by telephoning DSA's Policy Section on tel. 0115 901 5918.

New additional MTV requirements for vehicles brought into first use after 1 October 2003

Category	Description
C1	Minimum length 5 metres, MAM of at least 4 tonnes. The cargo compartment of the vehicle shall consist of a closed box body which is at least as wide and high as the cab.
C1 + E	Minimum MAM 4 tonnes (2 tonne trailer). The cargo compartment of the trailer shall consist of a closed box body which is at least as wide and high as the cab. The closed box body may be narrower than the tractor vehicle, provided that the driver's view to the rear of the trailer is only made posible by the use of the external rear-view mirrors of the tractor vehicle. The overall vehicle length should be at least 8 metres.
C	Minimum MAM 12 tonnes, minimum length 8 metres and minimum width 2.4 metres. The cargo compartment of the vehicle shall consist of a closed box body which is at least as wide and high as the cab. The vehicle must have at least eight forward gear ratios.
C + E	Articulated lorry: minimum MAM 20 tonnes, minimum length 14 metres and minimum width 2.4 metres
	Draw-bar trailer: minimum MAM 20 tonnes, minimum length 14 metres (minimum length of trailer 7.5 metres) and minimum width 2.4 metres. The relevant cargo compartment of the articulated goods vehicle combination or the trailer shall consist of a closed box body which is at least as wide and high as the cab. The vehicle must have at least eight forward gear ratios.

Test vehicles in all categories must be fitted with an anti-lock braking system and a tachograph.

Cone positions

Ready reckoner: metric measurements

This list of metric measurements should prove useful if you want to practise the reversing exercise.

To calculate the reversing area's layout identify the length of your vehicle in the left-hand columns and scan across to the right-hand columns for the relevant cone measurements. The cone positions are relative to the base line Z (see Diagram on page 178).

Metres	Feet	Cone A	Cone B
4.50	14.8	22.5	13.5
4.75	15.6	23.8	14.3
5.00	16.4	25.0	15.0
5.25	17.2	26.3	15.8
5.50	18.0	27.5	16.5
5.75	18.9	28.8	17.3
6.00	19.7	30.0	18.0
6.25	20.5	31.3	18.8
6.50	21.3	32.5	19.5
6.75	22.1	33.8	20.3
7.00	23.0	35.0	21.0
7.25	23.8	36.3	21.8
7.50	24.6	37.5	22.5
7.75	25.4	38.8	23.3
8.00	26.2	40.0	24.0
8.25	27.1	41.3	24.8
8.50	27.9	42.5	25.5
8.75	28.7	43.8	26.3
9.00	29.5	45.0	27.0
9.25	30.3	46.3	27.8
9.50	31.2	47.5	28.5
9.75	32.0	48.8	29.3
10.00	32.8	50.0	30.0
10.25	33.6	51.3	30.8
10.50	34.4	52.5	31.5
10.75	35.3	53.8	32.3
11.00	36.1	55.0	33.0
11.25	36.9	56.3	33.8
11.50	37.7	57.5	34.5
11.75	38.5	58.8	35.3
12.00	39.4	60.0	36.0
12.25	40.2	61.3	36.8
12.50	41.0	62.5	37.5
12.75	41.8	63.8	38.3
13.00	42.7	65.0	39.0
13.25	43.5	66.3	39.8
13.50	44.3	67.5	40.5
13.75	45.1	68.8	41.3
14.00	45.9	70.0	42.0
14.25	46.8	71.3	42.8
14.50	47.6	72.5	43.5
14.75	48.4	73.8	44.3
15.00	49.2	75.0	45.0
15.25	50.0	76.3	45.8
15.50	50.9	77.5	46.5
15.75	51.7	78.8	47.3
16.00	52.5	80.0	48.0
16.25	53.3	81.3	48.8
16.50	54.1	82.5	49.5
16.75	55.0	83.8	50.3
17.00	55.8	85.0	51.0
17.25	56.6	86.3	51.8
17.50	57.4	87.5	52.5
17.75	58.2	88.8	53.3
18.00	59.1	90.0	54.0
18.25	59.9	91.3	54.8

Glossary

A **ABS** Anti-lock braking system (developed by Bosch) which uses electronic sensors to detect when a wheel is about to lock, releases the brakes sufficiently to allow the wheel to revolve, then repeats the process in a very short space of time – thus avoiding skidding.

ADR Abbreviation used for European rules for the transport of hazardous materials by road.

Air suspension system This uses a compressible material (usually air), contained in chambers located between the axle and the vehicle body, to replace normal steel-leaf spring suspension. Gives an even load height (empty or laden) and added protection to fragile goods in transit.

Axle weights Limits laid down for maximum permitted weights carried by each axle – depending on axle spacings and wheel/tyre arrangement. (Consult regulations, charts or publications that give the legal requirements.)

B **BS EN ISO 9000** British Standards code relating to quality assurance adopted by vehicle body-builders, recovery firms, etc.

C **C & U (Regs)** Construction and Use regulations that set out specifications that govern the design and use of goods vehicles.

CAG Computer-aided gearshift system developed by Scania that employs an electronic control unit combined with electropneumatic actuators and a mechanical gearbox. The clutch is still required to achieve the gear change using an electrical gear lever switch.

City of London Security Regulations Anti-terrorist measures which mean that access to the City of London is restricted to only seven access points, involving closure of several other roads. Full details can be obtained from the Metropolitan Police.

COSHH Regulations 1988 The Control of Substances Hazardous to Health Regulations 1988 place a responsibility on employers to make a proper assessment of the effects of the storage or use of any substances that may represent a risk to their employees' health. (Details can be obtained from the Health and Safety Executive.)

CPC Certificate of Professional Competence indicates that the holder has attained the standards of knowledge required in order to exercise proper control of a transport business (and is required before an operator's licence can be granted).

Cruise control A facility that allows a vehicle to travel at a set speed without use of the accelerator pedal. However, the driver can immediately return to normal control by pressing the accelerator or brake pedal.

D **Diff-lock** A device by which the driver can arrange for the power to be transmitted to both wheels on an axle (normally rotating at different speeds when the vehicle is cornering, for example), which increases traction on surfaces such as mud, snow, etc.

Double de-clutching A driving technique that enables the driver to adjust the engine revs to the road speed when changing gear. The clutch pedal is released briefly while the gear lever is in the 'neutral' position. When changing down, engine revs are increased to match the engine speed to the lower gear in order to minimise the work load being placed on the synchro-mesh mechanism.

Drive-by-wire Modern electronic control systems that replace direct mechanical linkages.

E **Electronic engine management system** This system monitors and controls both fuel supply to the engine and the contents of the exhaust gases produced. The system is an essential part of some speed-retarder systems.

Electronic power shift A semi-automatic transmission system, developed by Mercedes, that requires the clutch to be fully depressed each time a gear change is made. This system then selects the appropriate gear.

G **GCW** Gross combination weight, applying to articulated vehicles.

Geartronic A fully automated transmission system developed by Volvo. There's no clutch pedal. Instead, there's an additional pedal operating the exhaust brake.

GTW Gross train weight, applying to drawbar combinations.

GVW Gross vehicle weight, applying to solo rigid vehicles and tractor units.

H **HSE** The Health and Safety Executive. HSE produces literature that provides advice and information on health and safety issues at work.

I **Inter-modal operations** Combined road and rail operations for the movement of goods where the 44 tonnes weight limit is authorised – subject to certain conditions.

J **Jake brake** A long-established system of speed retarding that alters the valve timing in the engine. In effect, the engine becomes a compressor and holds back the vehicle's speed.

K **Kerb weight** The total weight of a vehicle plus fuel, excluding any load (or driver).

L **Laminated** A process where plastic film is sandwiched between two layers of glass so that an object upon striking a windscreen, for example, will normally indent the screen without large fragments of glass causing injury to the driver.

Lifting axle An axle that may be lowered or raised, depending on whether the load is required to be distributed to include the additional axle or the vehicle is running unladen. Such axles may be driven, steered or free-running.

LNG Liquified (compressed) Natural Gas.

Load-sensing valve A valve in an air brake system that can be adjusted to reduce the possibility of wheels locking when the vehicle is unladen.

London lorry ban Night-time and weekend ban on lorries over 16.5 tonnes MAM, applying to most roads in Greater London other than trunk roads and exempted roads. All vehicles other than special types or those concerned with safety or emergency operations must display a permit and exemption plate if they're to be used in the restricted areas.

Note

Not all London boroughs operate the scheme.

LPG Liquified (compressed) Petroleum Gas.

M **MAM** Maximum authorised mass, also known as maximum authorised weight or gross vehicle weight.

MPW Maximum permissible weight. Under the EC drivers' hours rules, the weight of the vehicle and that of any trailer (added together) or the towing vehicle's maximum permissible train weight, whichever is the less.

P **Plated** Department for Transport regulations for recording and displaying information relating to dimensions and weights of goods vehicles, indicating maximum gross weight, maximum axle weight and maximum train weight. In the case of trailers the plate indicates maximum gross weight and maximum axle weight for each axle. (This is in addition to any manufacturer's plate that's fixed to the vehicle or trailer.)

R **Range change** Gearbox arrangement that permits the driver to select a series of either high or low ratio gears depending on the load, speed and any gradient being negotiated. Effectively doubles the number of gears available (frequently up to a total of 16 gears, including crawler gears).

Red Routes Approximately 300 route miles in the London area have become subject to stringent regulations restricting stopping, unloading and loading.

Re-grooving A process permitted for use on tyres for vehicles over an unladen weight of 2,540 kg, allowing a new tread pattern to be cut into the existing tyre surface (subject to certain conditions).

Retarder An additional braking system that may be either mechanical or electrical. Mechanical devices either alter the engine exhaust gas flow or amend the valve timing (creating a 'compressor' effect). Electrical devices comprise an electromagnetic field energised around the transmission drive shaft (more frequently used on passenger vehicles).

S **SAMT** Semi-automatic transmission system in which the clutch is only used when starting off or stopping.

Selective or block change A sequence of gear-changing omitting intermediate gears. Sometimes known as selective gear-changing.

Splitter box Another name for a gearbox with high and low ratios that effectively doubles the number of gears available.

T **Tachograph** A recorder indicating vehicle speeds, duration of journey, rest stops, etc. Required to be fitted to specified vehicles.

TBV Initials of the French (Renault) semi-automatic transmission system that employs a selector lever plus visual display information.

TC Traffic Commissioner, appointed by the Secretary of State to a Traffic Area to act as the licensing authority for Goods Vehicle and PSV operators in the area.

Thinking gearbox The term used to describe a fully automated gearbox that selects the appropriate gear for the load, gradient and speed, etc. by means of electronic sensors.

Toughened safety glass The glass undergoes a heat treatment process during manufacture so that in the event of an impact (such as a stone) on the windscreen it breaks up into small blunt fragments, thus reducing the risk of injury. An area on the windscreen in front of the driver is designed to give a zone of vision in the event of such an impact.

Trailer swing This occurs when severe braking causes partial loss of control as the rear wheels of a semi-trailer lock up on an articulated vehicle.

Turbo-charged The exhaust gas drives a turbine, which compresses incoming air and effectively delivers more air to the engine than is the case with a normal or non-turbo-charged engine.

Turbo-cooled or intercooled Refers to a system where the air from the turbo-charger is cooled before being delivered to the engine. The cooling increases the density of the compressed air to further improve engine power and torque.

Two-speed axle A system whereby an electrical switch actuates a mechanism in the rear axle that doubles the number of ratios available to the driver.

U **Unloader valve** A device fitted to air brake systems, between the compressor and the storage reservoir, pre-set to operate as sufficient pressure is achieved and allowing the excess to be released (often heard at regular intervals when the engine is running).

V **VEL** Vehicle Excise Licence or road fund licence.

VRO Vehicle Registration Office, dealing with matters relating to registration of goods vehicles, taxation and licensing.

Hazard labels

Printed in the United Kingdom by The Stationery Office Limited
N176107 03/05 C40 302446 19585

Titles for professional LGV and PCV drivers

Prepare for the professional tests and a new career with the official guidance ...

The Official Guide to Hazard Perception

Essential for learner drivers, this official guide to hazard perception is aimed at all drivers and riders. The DVD or video and booklet pack helps you to understand the action of others and includes information specific to each vehicle type.

DVD ISBN 0 11 552494 0	£15.99 INC VAT	
VIDEO ISBN 0 11 552578 5	£12.99 INC VAT	

The Official Theory Test for Drivers of Large Vehicles

This is the only official theory test book for drivers of large vehicles. It contains all the questions you are likely to be asked, together with all the official explanations, theory test instruction, and advice on where and when the test can be taken.

BOOK ISBN 0 11 552451 7   £14.99

CD-ROM ISBN 0 11 552406 1   £35.00 INC VAT

Driving Buses and Coaches – the Official DSA Syllabus

A companion volume to *The Official Theory Test for Drivers of Large Vehicles*, covering every aspect of driving a passenger carrying vehicle (PCV). Contains the officially recommended PCV practical test syllabus, plus information on how to book and prepare for the test.

ISBN 0 11 552486 X   £14.99

The Highway Code

The Highway Code is essential reading for all road users. It explains road traffic law and gives guidance on best driving practice. The current version covers up-to-date issues such as driver fatigue and in-vehicle technology.

ISBN 0 11 552449 5   £1.49

5 easy ways to order:

- **Online:** Visit **www.tso.co.uk/dsa**

- **Tel:** Please call **0870 243 0123**
  textphone **0870 243 0701**

- **Fax:** Fax your order to **0870 243 0129**

- **Post:** **Marketing, TSO,**
  Freepost ANG 4748,
  Norwich NR3 1YX

- **Shops:** Visit your local TSO Bookshop
  or order at all good bookstores

Prices are correct at time of going to press but
may be subject to change without notice.